the slow cooker cookbook

the slow cooker cookbook

GINA STEER

A QUINTET BOOK

Published by Apple Press
7 Greenland Street
London
NW1 0ND

www.apple-press.com

ISBN-13: 978-1-84092-332-2

This book was designed and produced by
Quintet Publishing Limited
6 Blundell Street
London N7 9BH

SLCC

Project Editor: Corinne Masciocchi
Editor: Deborah Gray
Art Director: Sharanjit Dhol
Designers: Rod Teasdale and Carmel O'Neil
Photographer: Ian Garlick
Food Stylist: Justine Kiggen
Creative Director: Richard Dewing
Publisher: Oliver Salzmann

Colour separation in China by Regent Publishing Services Limited
Printed in China by SNP Leefung Printers Ltd

CREDITS

Thanks are due to my family and friends who have eaten every one of these recipes,
both praising and suggesting improvements where they considered necessary. A very big
thank you to Ian Garlick for the stunning photography, and Justine Kiggen, the food stylist.

The Publishers wish to thank Russell Hobbs for the use of their slow cookers in the
preparation of all the dishes in this book.

CONTENTS

Christmas Grog

INTRODUCTION

Once you've become used to life with a slow cooker, you cannot imagine life without one. Its versatility is immense, the flavour of the food divine and it is incredibly simple to use. But you probably know this; otherwise, why would you buy this book? However, if your cooker is still sitting in its box in the cupboard, pull it out, shake off the dust and get cooking!

There are many advantages to using a slow cooker. One of the best is without doubt the way the flavours develop during the long, slow cooking, resulting in an explosion of tastes unimaginable before. The tenderness of the meat is amazing, and this applies to even the cheapest cuts, with the added bonus that all the nutrients of the food cooked in this way are retained. Fish and vegetables, too, take on a completely different taste with none of the flavours lost. Fruit desserts are delicious, chutneys and relishes are full of flavour and ready to eat immediately, no need to leave to mature.

In addition, you do not need to worry that your pot is going to burn dry or that you are using too much fuel. The slow cooker is environmentally friendly, saving up to two-thirds of fuel normally used in a conventional oven. However, there are a few guidelines to bear in mind when first starting to use your cooker.

FOOD PREPARATION

In many of the recipes, the meat or vegetables are seared by frying lightly in a frying pan or saucepan before placing in the cooker. This is to help with the appearance, texture and flavour. However, it is not strictly necessary, and if you have very little preparation time it is possible to skip this step. Likewise, many of the soups have been puréed for a smooth texture and appearance, but again this is a matter of personal taste.

Frozen foods should be thoroughly thawed before being placed in the cooker, and the cooking time for these is less than for their fresh counterparts. Normally, thawed frozen vegetables or shellfish are added towards the end of the cooking time.

Dried beans should be soaked in cold water overnight or for at least eight hours before cooking in the slow cooker. Some beans, such as kidney beans, must be boiled for 10 minutes in order to kill toxins contained in the bean – check on the package if in doubt. Lentils, however, do not need pre-soaking. With rice, use the easy-cook or converted rice as these are partially cooked and much of the starch has been removed, reducing the risk of the finished rice sticking together. It is always a good idea to rinse the rice before using. Pasta is best added about 40 minutes before the end of the total cooking time. Root vegetables take longer to cook than meat or fish, so it is important that they are cut into smaller pieces than normal and completely covered with the cooking liquid.

A better flavour is achieved with the use of dried rather than fresh herbs during the long, slow cooking – fresh herbs can be sprinkled on just before serving to enhance the flavour and appearance of the finished dish.

You can thicken the dish either at the beginning or at the end of the cooking time. Either use flour at the beginning, when searing the meat or vegetables, or stir in cornflour towards the end. You will need to use a little more flour or cornflour than normal if you prefer a thick sauce because, due to the long, slow cooking, the volume of liquid is increased.

COOKER SETTINGS

The slow cooker is controlled by four switches: off, low, high, and auto. At the low setting, the cooker will cook at its lowest temperature. When this setting is used, the cooker needs to be preheated on high for 20 minutes. The power light will be on the entire time.

With the high setting, the red light will also stay on the entire time and the cooker will cook at its highest power. If by the remotest chance the food does dry out, do not simply add cold liquid; switch off, unplug, then add warm or cold water – you can then continue cooking.

With the auto cook function, cooking starts at a high temperature, then automatically switches to low cook. The temperature is thermostatically controlled and the light will

▲ Slow cookers have various temperature settings. Please ensure you check the manufacturer's guidelines first.

come on and off. With this facility it is possible to cook during the night, allowing you to cook tomorrow's breakfast or lunch overnight.

Best of all, you can set the cooker before you go to work and come home to a delicious home-cooked meal. Prepare the ingredients the night before and leave them overnight in the refrigerator (or you can forego searing the meat or vegetables beforehand). Whichever approach you take, place the empty cooking pot in the slow cooker and place the lid in position. Plug in and switch on and set the control to high. Preheat for 20 minutes and use this time to bring the cooking liquid to the boil. Once the cooker is heated, remove the lid, add the food to the cooking pot, then pour over the boiling liquid, cover with the lid and switch the cooker to auto cook. It is that simple.

All the recipes give instructions for preheating the cooker. This is important. Your manufacturer's booklet will give instructions for the cooker you have, so do refer to it.

When adapting your own recipes to cook in the slow cooker, simply look for similar recipes in the book and adapt cooking times accordingly.

TYPES OF COOKERS

Slow cookers vary in shape, size and capacity. So when choosing one there are a few points to bear in mind. All cookers have a low wattage and all consume about the same amount of electricity. The settings vary according to the make and size, so if buying a new cooker, choose one that will meet your needs. Those with an on/off switch have the distinct advantage of preventing the cooker from accidentally switching off during the cooking process.

It is possible to buy an earthenware pot that is permanently fixed into an outer casing normally made of aluminium or heat resistant plastic. Heating elements are placed around the outside of the inner pot between the outer casing and the cooking pot. It is possible to obtain cookers that have a detachable cord to enable the cooker to be taken to the table.

Another type of cooker has a removable inner earthenware cooking pot, which means that only the cooking pot needs to be taken to the table. Food can easily be browned or crisped under the grill using only the cooking pot, thus ensuring the outer casing is not damaged by the heated grill elements. In such cookers the heating elements are fitted within the outer casing located either on the base or sides.

There are different capacity cookers that vary from 1.5 to 3.5 litres/3 to 8 pints. It is a good idea to buy a large rather than a small cooker, as it enables you to cook a far greater range of dishes and to cater for more people.

COOKER CARE

Looking after your cooker is simple but very important. Before you use your cooker for the first time, wash in mild soapy water, rinse and dry thoroughly. After use, remove the cooking pot and empty out the food (take care when handling the hot pot; use oven mitts). After emptying, do not immediately plunge into cold or boiling water. Switch off, unplug and fill the cooking pot with warm water. Then wash as before in warm soapy water and rinse well.

If necessary, soak for a few minutes to remove any stubborn pieces of food, then gently brush with a soft brush. Dry thoroughly. Do not leave the cooking pot immersed in water, as the porous base could crack when heated. NEVER immerse the outer casing in water, fill with water or use the outer casing for cooking without the inner cooking pot. If the outer casing needs cleaning, wipe clean with a mild detergent, such as washing-up liquid. The lid should also be thoroughly washed, ensuring that the small vent hole is free from any food particles. Do not put any part of the cooker in the dishwasher or use harsh abrasive cleaners, which could damage the finish.

GENERAL TIPS

► Check when cooking joints, puddings or foods cooked in dishes such as pudding basins or gratin dishes that the food or dishes fit comfortably in the cooking pot and that the lid fits securely.

► Root vegetables take longer to cook than meat or fish, so cut them up into small bite-sized pieces and place in the base of the cooker, completely covering with liquid.

► When browning meat it can be a good idea to brown the vegetables as well. Frozen vegetables, fish, shellfish, meat or poultry should be completely thawed before using.

► Use easy-cook or converted rice and dried pasta, rinsing the rice before use. Add the pasta towards the end of the cooking time. If the cooker has a removable cooking pot, finished dishes can be browned or crisped under the grill.

► Thicken the liquids either at the beginning or at the end. Remember that this method of cooking can produce more liquid, so if thick sauces are preferred, use more thickener than when cooking conventionally. Use flour at the beginning of cooking and cornflour at the end. If the dish is cooked on the low setting, blend the cornflour with water, stir into the cooking pot, turn the setting up to high and cook for 20-30 minutes.

► Do not over-season at the beginning of cooking. This applies especially to ham. It is easy to add salt and pepper at the end of cooking, but over-seasoning is hard to rectify. Should this happen, add a little sweetener such as maple syrup or clear honey to balance the flavour or add some plain mashed potatoes, which will absorb some of the seasoning.

► Milk and cream are best added towards the end or at the end of cooking time to prevent curdling.

► All whole joints of meat should be cooked on high and all poultry is also best cooked on high to kill off any toxins that may be present.

► When using minced meat, drain off any excess fat after browning, if necessary. Likewise, skim the fat from the juices produced by meat and poultry after cooking using a brush or spoon, or soak up with a slice of bread.

► Cookers should be at least half-full and no more than three-quarters full.

► When adapting your own recipe, you will find that there is probably too much liquid in the conventional recipe, so cut the liquid in half.

► Always use liquid in your cooker. Dishes such as baked potatoes are not suitable.

► A good guide to gauging cooking times is that one hour on the high setting is equal to $2\frac{1}{2}$ hours of low cooking. So if you want to cook a dish that is written for low cooking and you want to speed up the cooking process, simply use this as a guide and cook on high.

► Where the recipe states cook for 4 to 6 hours, this means that the food is cooked in four hours and will keep for a further two hours. Once cooked and on hold, it is a good idea to check the food occasionally and see if it needs to be stirred. But if you keep peeping during the actual cooking time, every time you lift the lid you set the cooking time back 15 minutes. This time will have to be added to the final cooking time.

► A slow cooker is a real asset – it will make life so much easier. Enjoy using it and make it work for you.

1

STARTERS AND SAUCES

SMOKED HADDOCK AND BROAD BEAN CHOWDER

THIS SOUP IS DEFINITELY BETTER IF YOU REMOVE THE BROAD BEANS FROM THEIR TOUGH OUTER SKINS. IT MAY BE A LITTLE TIME CONSUMING BUT WELL WORTH THE EFFORT.

SERVES	PREPARATION TIME	COOKING TIME	AUTO COOK
4	25 minutes	Cook on low 5 to 6 hours	6 to 9 hours

25 g/1 oz unsalted butter

1 medium onion, peeled and chopped

350 g/12 oz new potatoes, scrubbed and diced

1 tbsp flour

450 ml/¾ pt vegetable stock

300 g/10 oz smoked haddock fillet, skinned and diced

150 ml/¼ pt semi-skimmed milk

Freshly ground black pepper

75 g/3oz sweetcorn kernels, thawed if frozen

100 g/4 oz broad beans, removed from skins, thawed if frozen

1 tbsp freshly chopped parsley

2–3 tbsp soured cream

Crusty bread, to serve

1 Preheat the cooker on high. Melt the butter in a pan; then sauté the onion and potatoes for 3 minutes, stirring frequently. Sprinkle in the flour and cook for 2 minutes; then take the pan off the heat. Gradually stir in the stock and bring to the boil. Add the diced smoked haddock with the milk and a little freshly ground black pepper.

2 Spoon or pour into the cooking pot, cover and reduce the temperature to low. Cook for 4 hours. Mix the corn and broad beans together then add to the cooking pot and continue to cook for an additional 1 to 2 hours.

3 Stir in the chopped parsley, adjust the seasoning and serve with spoonfuls of soured cream and chunks of crusty bread.

SUNBURST SOUP

THE ADVANTAGE OF COOKING SOUP IN THE SLOW COOKER IS THAT THERE IS NO
DANGER OF THE SOUP BURNING – THE FLAVOUR JUST CONTINUES TO IMPROVE.

SERVES	PREPARATION TIME	COOKING TIME	AUTO COOK
6	35 minutes	Cook on low 6 to 8 hours	6 to 10 hours

3 medium red peppers

1 tbsp oil

1 medium onion, peeled and finely chopped

2–3 garlic cloves, peeled and crushed

1 red serrano chilli, deseeded and chopped

3 ripe plum tomatoes

900 ml/1½ pt vegetable or chicken stock

1 tsp soft brown sugar

Salt and freshly ground black pepper

Few sprigs fresh basil

4 tbsp soured cream

Freshly chopped basil, to garnish

Warm Italian bread, to serve

1 Preheat the cooker on high. Cut the peppers in half, deseed and remove membranes, then place under a preheated grill and cook for 10 minutes, turning, or until the skins have charred slightly. Remove from the heat, place in a paper bag and leave for 10 minutes. When cool enough to handle, skin the peppers and slice thinly.

2 Meanwhile, heat the oil in a large pan and sauté the onion, garlic and serrano chilli for 5 minutes, stirring frequently. Roughly chop the tomatoes and add to the onions together with the sliced peppers and sauté for 2 minutes. Add the stock with the sugar and seasoning to taste. Bring to the boil, pour into the slow cooker and add a few basil sprigs. Cook on low for 6 to 8 hours. If a smoother soup is preferred, cool slightly, then blend and reheat gently. Swirl with the cream, garnish with the chopped basil and serve accompanied by the bread.

DUCK PÂTÉ

THIS PÂTÉ FREEZES WELL AND DOES NOT CHANGE IN TEXTURE ON THAWING. IT IS
A GREAT RECIPE TO MAKE REGULARLY AND FREEZE FOR ENTERTAINING.

MAKES	PREPARATION TIME	COOKING TIME
12 slices	20 minutes	Cook on high 4 to 6 hours

200 g/7 oz Parma ham, or prosciutto

675 g/1½ lb duck breast meat

450 g/1 lb turkey breast meat

100 g/4 oz bacon

Grated rind and juice of 1 large orange

4 shallots, peeled and finely chopped

1 garlic clove, peeled and crushed

Salt and freshly ground black pepper

2 tbsp chopped fresh parsley

¼ tsp freshly grated nutmeg

2 tbsp brandy

2 tbsp orange marmalade

3–4 fresh bay leaves

1 small orange and fresh cherries, to garnish

1 Preheat the cooker on high. Take a 1.2-litre/2-pint ovenproof dish that will sit in the top of the cooking pot and line the base and sides with the Parma ham, allowing the ham to fall over the sides of the dish. Remove and discard the fat from the duck breasts and cut into very small pieces. Trim the turkey and cut into small cubes. Chop the bacon. Either finely chop in a food processor or mincer and place in a bowl.

2 Add the orange rind and juice with the shallots, garlic, seasoning, parsley and nutmeg. Mix well together, then stir in the brandy. Spoon into the lined dish, pressing down with a spoon, and fold the ham over. Cover with tinfoil.

3 Place in the cooking pot and pour in sufficient hot water to come almost to the top. Cook on high for 4 to 6 hours. Remove and cool before turning out. Heat the marmalade and pass through a strainer. Arrange the bay leaves, orange and cherries on top of the pâté and brush with the smooth marmalade.

MINESTRONE SOUP

CHOOSE YOUR FAVOURITE BEANS FOR THIS SOUP – IF USING DRIED BEANS, SOAK THEM OVERNIGHT OR THEY MAY BE TOUGH. IF YOU OPT FOR CANNED BEANS, DRAIN AND RINSE, THEN ADD TO THE COOKER AFTER SAUTÉING THE ONIONS.

SERVES	PREPARATION TIME	COOKING TIME	AUTO COOK
4 to 6	30 minutes	Cook on low 6 to 8 hours	6 to 10 hours

1 tbsp olive oil

1 medium onion, peeled and chopped

3 garlic cloves, peeled and crushed

2 celery sticks, trimmed and finely diced

100 g/4 oz bacon, chopped

2 medium carrots, peeled and diced

1 large leek, thoroughly washed, trimmed and thinly sliced

450-g/16-oz can borlotti or haricot beans, drained and rinsed

900 ml/1½ pt vegetable stock

2 tbsp tomato purée

Salt and freshly ground black pepper

50 g/2 oz uncooked spaghetti

175 g/6 oz shredded green cabbage

Freshly grated Parmesan cheese and warm chunks of Italian bread, to serve

1 Preheat the slow cooker on high. Heat the oil in a large pan and sauté the onion, garlic, celery, bacon, carrots and leeks for 5 minutes, stirring frequently. Add the drained beans with the stock and the tomato purée blended with 2 tablespoons of water. Bring to the boil. Pour into the cooker, add seasoning, then cook for 5 hours.

2 Break the spaghetti into small lengths, add to the slow cooker and continue to cook for another hour, adding the cabbage for the last 30 minutes of cooking time. Check seasoning. Serve with Parmesan cheese and bread.

TOMATO AND BASIL SOUP

ALTHOUGH IT IS BETTER TO USE DRIED HERBS, DRIED BASIL IS NOT INTENSE
IN FLAVOUR, SO ADD FRESH BASIL TOWARDS THE END OF COOKING.

SERVES	PREPARATION TIME	COOKING TIME	AUTO COOK
4	15 minutes	Cook on low 8 to 10 hours	10 to 12 hours

6 sundried tomatoes, chopped

1 tbsp olive oil

1 red onion, peeled and chopped

2–3 garlic cloves, peeled and crushed

450 g/1 lb skinned, chopped
ripe plum tomatoes

1 red pepper, skinned, deseeded
and chopped

1 tbsp grated orange rind

150 ml/¼ pt orange juice

1 tsp sugar

600 ml/1 pint vegetable stock

Salt and freshly ground black pepper

Few basil sprigs

3–4 tbsp soured cream

1 tbsp freshly shredded basil

Shaved fresh Parmesan cheese

1 tbsp cornflour, optional

Warm Italian bread, to serve

1 Preheat the slow cooker on high. Cover the sundried tomatoes with almost boiling water and leave for 10 minutes. Then drain, reserving the soaking liquor.

2 Heat the olive oil in a pan, then gently sauté the sundried tomatoes, onion and garlic for 4 minutes. Add the chopped plum tomatoes with the red pepper and continue to cook, stirring frequently, for 5 minutes. Add the soaking liquor with the grated orange rind, juice, sugar, stock with seasoning to taste, and bring to the boil.

3 Add the basil sprigs and then pour the soup into the cooking pot. Reduce the temperature to low, cover and cook for 8 to 10 hours. Blend the soup until smooth, adjust seasoning and serve immediately with spoonfuls of soured cream topped with the shredded basil and Parmesan cheese. Alternatively, for a thicker soup, blend the cornflour with 2 tablespoons of water, stir into the soup and pour into a pan. Cook, stirring, until the soup has thickened slightly, then serve as above with chunks of warm Italian bread.

SWEET POTATO VICHYSSOISE

THIS SOUP CAN BE SERVED HOT OR CHILLED. IF SERVING COLD, IT NEEDS TO BE
CHILLED FOR AT LEAST 4 HOURS. GARNISH JUST BEFORE SERVING.

SERVES	PREPARATION TIME	COOKING TIME	AUTO COOK
4 to 6	20 minutes	Cook on low 6 to 8 hours	8 to 10 hours

900 ml/1½ pt chicken stock

1 medium white onion, peeled and
finely chopped

2 garlic cloves, peeled and crushed

1–2 red jalapeño chillies, deseeded
and chopped

450 g/1 lb sweet potatoes, peeled
and cut into chunks

1 ripe mango, peeled, pitted
and chopped

Salt and freshly ground black pepper

120 ml/4 fl oz single cream

4 spring onions, trimmed and
finely chopped

1 tbsp chopped fresh coriander

1 Preheat the cooker on high while preparing the ingredients. Place the chicken stock with the onion, garlic, chillies, sweet potatoes and mango in the cooking pot with a little seasoning. Cover with the lid and cook on low for 6 to 8 hours.

2 Cool slightly, purée, then, if serving hot, return either to the cleaned cooking pot or to a clean pan. Stir in the cream, adjust the seasoning and either heat for 1 hour in the slow cooker, or heat on the stove for 5 to 10 minutes, until hot but not boiling. Stir in the chopped spring onions and coriander and serve. If serving chilled, after puréeing, stir in the cream, adjust seasoning, then stir in the chopped spring onions and coriander. Chill for at least 4 hours, then stir before serving.

LENTIL AND SQUASH BROTH

THIS BROTH IS IDEAL TO SERVE WHEN THE WEATHER IS BEGINNING TO TURN
COLD OR A BOWL OF COMFORT FOOD IS REQUIRED.

SERVES	PREPARATION TIME	COOKING TIME	AUTO COOK
6	25 minutes	Cook on low 6 to 8 hours	8 to 10 hours

25 g/1 oz unsalted butter

1 small butternut or harlequin squash,
    about 450 g/1 lb, peeled, deseeded
    and chopped

3 celery stalks, trimmed and chopped

1 onion, peeled and chopped

¼–1 tsp dried, crushed chillies

100 g/4 oz red lentils

2 tbsp tomato purée

1.2 l/ 2 pt vegetable stock

Salt and freshly ground black pepper

Fresh coriander sprigs

Freshly grated hard cheese, such as
    Cheddar or Monterey Jack, to serve

1 Preheat the cooker on high. Melt the butter in a large pan and sauté
the squash, chopped celery, onion and crushed chillies for 5 minutes.
Add the lentils and cook, stirring, for 2 more minutes.

2 Blend the tomato purée with a little of the stock, add to the pan, stir,
then pour in the remaining stock. Bring to the boil, add a little
seasoning, then pour or spoon into the cooking pot.

3 Reduce the temperature to low, cover and cook for 6 to 8 hours.
When ready to serve, blend the soup until smooth and adjust
seasoning. Reheat if necessary and serve, sprinkling with a little
cheese and garnish with fresh coriander sprigs.

TURKEY AND RICE CHOWDER

THIS CHOWDER IS A MEAL IN ITSELF. USE EASY-COOK RICE AS THIS MAKES A
DIFFERENCE TO THE FINISHED DISH AND REMEMBER TO RINSE THE RICE FIRST.

SERVES	PREPARATION TIME	COOKING TIME	AUTO COOK
6	25 minutes	Cook on low 5 to 7 hours	7 to 10 hours

25 g/1 oz unsalted butter

1 medium onion, peeled and chopped

2 garlic cloves, peeled and crushed

1 green jalapeño chilli, deseeded and
    chopped

225 g/8 oz skinned, boned turkey
    breast steak, finely chopped

50 g/2 oz easy-cook rice, rinsed

2 carrots, peeled and finely diced

75 g/3 oz baby corn, chopped

1 orange pepper, deseeded and
    chopped

1 red pepper, deseeded and chopped

1.2 l/2 pt turkey or chicken stock

Salt and freshly ground black pepper

¼ tsp freshly grated nutmeg

75 g/3 oz shelled peas, thawed if frozen

1 tbsp chopped fresh tarragon

3–5 tbsp single cream

Warm crusty bread, to serve

1 Preheat the cooker on high. Melt the butter in a large pan and sauté
the onion, garlic and chilli for 3 minutes. Add the chopped turkey and
continue to sauté for another 3 minutes or until seared. Add the rice
and cook for 2 minutes before adding the carrots, baby corn and
peppers. Pour in the stock, add seasoning with the grated nutmeg
and bring to the boil.

2 Pour or ladle the soup into the cooking pot, cover and reduce the
temperature to low. Cook for 4 hours, then stir in the peas and
continue to cook for 1 hour. Add the chopped tarragon and cream,
then adjust seasoning to taste. Reheat if necessary. Serve with
chunks of warm crusty bread.

WILD MUSHROOM AND CHILLI SOUP

WHEN USING DRIED MUSHROOMS, IT IS IMPORTANT THAT THEY ARE ALLOWED TO SOAK IN HOT BUT NOT BOILING WATER AS THIS MAY IMPAIR THEIR FLAVOUR.

SERVES	PREPARATION TIME	COOKING TIME	AUTO COOK
4	20 minutes plus 20 minutes soaking	Cook on low 4 to 5 hours	5 to 8 hours

1 tbsp dried porcini mushrooms

2 tbsp olive oil

1–2 fresh red jalapeño chillies, deseeded and chopped

2–3 garlic cloves, peeled and chopped

4 shallots, peeled and finely chopped

225 g/8 oz potatoes, peeled and diced

225 g/8 oz assorted wild mushrooms, such as chanterelles, oyster and girolles, wiped clean

100 g/4 oz sliced button mushrooms, wiped clean

1 tbsp flour

600 ml/1 pt vegetable or chicken stock

Salt and freshly ground black pepper

150 ml/¼ pt soured cream

Flat leaf parsley sprigs, to garnish

Warm Italian bread, to serve

1 Soak the porcini in hot but not boiling water for at least 20 minutes and drain, reserving the liquor. Preheat the cooker on high. Heat the oil in a large pan and sauté the chilli, garlic, shallots and potatoes for 5 minutes. Cut any large wild mushrooms into small pieces. Add to the pan with the drained porcini and the button mushrooms and sauté for 2 minutes. Sprinkle in the flour and cook for 2 minutes, then gradually stir in the stock. Strain the reserved soaking liquor and add to the pan with a little seasoning.

2 Bring to the boil, then spoon or pour into the cooking pot. Cover and reduce the temperature to low and cook for 4 to 5 hours.

3 Cool slightly, then blend until smooth, stir in the soured cream and adjust seasoning to taste. Reheat if necessary. Serve, garnished with parsley and accompanied by chunks of warm Italian bread.

CHICKEN CLAM CHOWDER

THE POTATOES NEED TO BE COMPLETELY COVERED WITH THE STOCK TO ENSURE THAT THEY ARE THOROUGHLY COOKED.

SERVES	PREPARATION TIME	COOKING TIME	AUTO COOK
4 to 6	15 minutes	Cook on low 6 to 8 hours	7 to 12 hours

225 g/8 oz gammon, diced

1 large onion, peeled and chopped

2 celery sticks, trimmed and chopped

2 medium potatoes, peeled and diced

2 boneless, skinless chicken thighs, about 300 g/10 oz, diced

750 ml/1¼ pt chicken stock

Salt and freshly ground black pepper

300 g/10 oz canned clams

175 g/6 oz sweetcorn kernels, thawed if frozen

6 tbsp single cream

2 tbsp chopped fresh parsley

Crusty bread or cornmeal bread, to serve

1 Preheat the slow cooker on high. Place the gammon in a large pan and heat gently, stirring, until the fat begins to run. Add the onion, celery and potatoes and continue to sauté for 3 minutes. Add the diced chicken and continue to cook, stirring frequently, until seared. Stir in the stock and seasoning to taste, then bring to the boil.

2 Pour into the cooking pot, cover and reduce the temperature to low. Cook for 5 hours. Add the clams with their juice and sweetcorn kernels and continue to cook for 1 to 3 hours. Stir in the cream with the parsley, adjust seasoning and serve with crusty bread or cornmeal bread.

LEEK AND LIME VICHYSSOISE

LEMON GRASS IMPARTS A DISTINCTIVE CITRUS FLAVOUR WHICH IS SIMILAR TO THAT OF A LEMON YET HAS A SLIGHTLY PERFUMED AROMA. IF UNAVAILABLE, USE 1 TABLESPOON OF GRATED LEMON RIND.

SERVES	PREPARATION TIME	COOKING TIME	AUTO COOK
4	25 minutes	Cook on low 5 to 6 hours	6 to 8 hours

2 lemon grass stalks

25 g/1 oz unsalted butter

2 medium leeks, thoroughly washed, trimmed and sliced

2–3 garlic cloves, peeled and chopped

350 g/12 oz potatoes, peeled and diced

1 tbsp grated lime rind

4 tbsp lime juice

900 ml/1½ pt vegetable or chicken stock

2 tbsp chopped fresh coriander

Salt and freshly ground black pepper

Green food colouring, optional

4 tbsp single cream

Toasted pitta bread, to serve

1 Preheat the cooker on high. Discard the outer leaves from the lemon grass stalks and finely chop the inner part. Melt the butter in a large pan and sauté the lemon grass, leeks, garlic and potatoes for 5 minutes, stirring frequently.

2 Add the lime rind and juice and cook for 2 more minutes. Then stir in the stock with half the chopped coriander and a little seasoning. Bring to the boil. Transfer to the cooking pot and cover with the lid.

3 Reduce the temperature to low and cook for 4 to 5 hours. Add the remaining chopped coriander, then cook for another hour. Blend the soup until smooth. Add a little green food colouring, if desired, and a little extra hot stock or water if the soup is too thick. Adjust seasoning and reheat if serving hot. Swirl with the cream and serve.

4 If serving chilled, chill in the refrigerator for at least 3 hours. Serve swirled with the cream and with toasted pitta bread.

CHEESY BEAN DIP

THIS DIP IS BEST IF SERVED WARM BECAUSE THE CHEESE TENDS TO HARDEN AS IT COOLS. IT REHEATS IN A MICROWAVE OR IN THE SLOW COOKER IF PREFERRED.

SERVES	PREPARATION TIME	COOKING TIME
6 to 8	15 minutes	Cook on high 1 hour

1 tsp oil

450-g/16-oz can refried beans

6 tbsp white wine or apple juice

1–3 red jalapeño chillies, deseeded and finely chopped

2–3 garlic cloves, peeled and crushed

300 g/10 oz grated Swiss cheese,

Corn chips, pretzels, vegetable crudités and cubes of bread, to serve

Preheat the cooker on high. Use the oil to wipe the cooking pot, then add the refried beans with the wine or apple juice and heat in the cooker until smooth, stirring occasionally. Stir in the chillies, garlic and cheese. Cover and cook on high for 1 hour or until the cheese has melted (it will keep on low for an extra 2 to 4 hours if not needed immediately). Stir until the mixture is smooth. Scrape down the sides of the cooker, then, if holding, reduce the temperature to low. Serve with the chips, pretzels, vegetable crudités and bread cubes.

FARMHOUSE TERRINE

BEFORE STARTING TO PREPARE THIS TERRINE, CHECK THAT THE DISH YOU ARE USING WILL FIT COMFORTABLY IN THE COOKING POT OF YOUR SLOW COOKER.

MAKES	PREPARATION TIME	COOKING TIME
10 to 12 slices	25 minutes	Cook on high 5 to 6 hours

150 g/5 oz bacon

1 tsp unsalted butter

3 garlic cloves, peeled and crushed

1 small onion, peeled and finely chopped

100 g/4 oz lamb's liver, chopped

350 g/12 oz pork fillet, minced

50 g/2 oz soft white breadcrumbs

2 tbsp chopped fresh mixed herbs

1 tbsp grated lemon rind

Salt and freshly ground black pepper

1 medium egg, beaten

2 tbsp brandy

Salad leaves or fresh herbs, to garnish

Melba toast and cranberry sauce, to serve

1 Preheat the cooker on high. Take a 1.2-litre/2-pint round pan or container that will sit in the cooking pot. Stretch the bacon rashers with the back of a knife, then use to line the pan or container, allowing the bacon rashers to fall over the sides.

2 Heat the butter in a pan and gently sauté the garlic and onion for 3 minutes. Add the liver and minced pork and cook for another 3 minutes or until seared all over.

3 Remove from the heat and stir in the breadcrumbs, herbs and the lemon rind, with seasoning to taste. Mix lightly, then add the egg and brandy and mix well.

4 Spoon into the bacon-lined pan, pressing the mixture down, then fold the bacon over the filling. Cover with tinfoil. Place in the cooking pot and pour boiling water around the pan to come nearly to the top of the pot. Cook on high for 5 to 6 hours. Remove, cool before turning out and garnish with salad leaves or herbs. Serve on Melba toast, spread with cranberry sauce.

CLASSIC RAGU SAUCE

THIS CLASSIC SAUCE CAN BE USED WITH FRESHLY COOKED SPAGHETTI OR TAGLIATELLE OR AS A BASIS FOR LASAGNE OR CANNELLONI. SPRINKLE WITH FRESHLY CHOPPED OREGANO OR MARJORAM AND FRESHLY GRATED PARMESAN.

SERVES	PREPARATION TIME	COOKING TIME	AUTO COOK
4	20 minutes	Cook on high 3 to 4 hours	4 to 8 hours

450 g/1 lb minced beef

1 tbsp oil

1 medium onion, peeled and chopped

2–4 garlic cloves, peeled and crushed

2 celery stalks, trimmed and chopped

2 medium carrots, peeled and diced

450-g/16-oz can chopped tomatoes

2 tbsp tomato purée

1 tsp mixed dried herbs

300 ml/½ pt red wine

Salt and freshly ground black pepper

1 Preheat the slow cooker on high. Place the minced beef in a non-stick frying pan and sauté for 5 minutes, stirring frequently until browned. Use a wooden spoon or spatula to break up any lumps. Remove from the heat and drain off any excess fat through a colander. Add the oil to the frying pan and sauté the onion, garlic, celery and carrots for 3 minutes, stirring, then return the beef to the pan. Add the remaining ingredients, stir well and bring to the boil.

2 Pour into the cooking pot of the cooker, cover and cook on high for 3 to 4 hours. Adjust seasoning and use as required.

BLACK BEAN CHILLI DIP

THIS RECIPE ALSO MAKES AN EXCELLENT FILLING FOR TACOS, WITH LETTUCE AND CUCUMBER, TOPPED WITH SOURED CREAM, SALSA AND GRATED CHEESE.

SERVES	PREPARATION TIME	COOKING TIME	AUTO COOK
6	20 minutes plus overnight soaking	Cook on low 8 to 10 hours	10 to 14 hours

225 g/8 oz dried black beans, soaked overnight

1 tbsp sunflower oil

1 large onion, peeled and chopped

2–4 garlic cloves, peeled and chopped

1–3 red serrano chillies, deseeded and chopped

1 large carrot, peeled and diced

1 red pepper, deseeded and chopped

450-g/16-oz can chopped tomatoes

175ml/6 fl oz vegetable stock

Salt and freshly ground black pepper

Hot chilli sauce, to taste

2 tbsp chopped fresh coriander

Warm pitta bread strips, sesame cheese straws and soured cream, to serve

1 Cover the black beans with cold water and leave to soak overnight. Next day, preheat the cooker on high. Drain the beans, place in a large pan, cover with cold water and bring to the boil. Boil steadily for 10 minutes, then drain and place in the cooking pot. Heat the oil in a frying pan and sauté the onion, garlic and chillies for 3 minutes. Remove from the heat and stir in the remaining ingredients except the seasoning, hot chilli sauce and freshly chopped coriander. Stir well, then spoon into the cooking pot of the cooker.

2 Cook on low for 8 to 10 hours. If necessary, strain off any excess liquid, then mash the beans to form a chunky consistency. Stir in the seasoning and hot chilli sauce to taste and sprinkle with the chopped coriander. Serve with warm pitta strips, sesame cheese straws and soured cream.

CHICKEN STOCK

POUR THE PREPARED STOCK INTO ICE CUBE TRAYS AND FREEZE, THEN POP INTO FREEZER BAGS TO STORE. USE AS REQUIRED.

MAKES	PREPARATION TIME	COOKING TIME
3¾ cups (900 ml)	10 minutes	Cook on high 2 hours then low 4 hours

1 chicken carcass, cut into pieces

1 onion, peeled and roughly chopped

1 carrot, peeled and roughly chopped

1 celery stalk, trimmed and roughly chopped

2 bay leaves

4–6 whole cloves

10 black peppercorns

Few fresh parsley stalks

1 Preheat the cooker on high. Rinse the chicken pieces, removing any stuffing, skin or fat, and place in the cooking pot. Add all the other ingredients plus 900 ml/1½ pints of water and cover with the lid. Cook on high for 2 hours, then reduce the temperature to low and cook for an additional 4 hours. Strain and skim. Store covered in the refrigerator and use as required.

2 The stock can be frozen and used within 1 month. If kept in the refrigerator, use within 3 days but take care that the stock is boiled for at least 3 minutes. To make a vegetable stock, omit the chicken carcass and increase the amount of vegetables. Do not use vegetables such as potato, which breaks up, or cabbage, which has a very strong flavour, as these may spoil the stock. Proceed as above.

3 Beef stock can also be made in the same way – break the bones if large into smaller pieces and, if raw, brown in a frying pan. Place in the cooking pot and proceed as above.

▶ Black Bean Chilli Dip

MEXICAN DIP

THESE DAYS IT SEEMS THAT EVERY TIME YOU VISIT FRIENDS THERE ARE A VARIETY OF DIFFERENT DIPS TO TRY – TRY SERVING THIS ONE TO CREATE AN IMPRESSION.

SERVES	PREPARATION TIME	COOKING TIME
6 to 8	15 minutes	Cook on high 2 to 4 hours

1 tbsp sunflower oil

1 white onion, peeled and finely chopped

1–3 jalapeño chillies, deseeded and chopped

2–3 garlic cloves, peeled and crushed

350 g/12 oz freshly minced turkey

1 tsp ground coriander

$\frac{1}{2}$ tsp ground cloves

4 tomatoes, peeled, if preferred, and chopped

1 green pepper, deseeded and finely chopped

Salt and freshly ground black pepper

100 g/4 oz canned green pickled chillies, chopped

225 g/8 oz cream cheese

1 tbsp chopped fresh coriander

Tortilla chips, to serve

Fresh coriander sprigs, to garnish

1 Preheat the cooker on high while preparing the ingredients. Heat the oil in a frying pan and sauté the onion, chillies and garlic for 3 minutes. Add the minced turkey and cook, stirring to break up the lumps, for 5 minutes, or until seared. Sprinkle in the spices and cook for 1 more minute, then add all the other ingredients except the chopped coriander and stir well.

2 Spoon into the cooking pot, cover with the lid and cook on high for 2 to 4 hours. Stir in the chopped coriander, garnish with fresh coriander sprigs and serve with tortilla chips. (If the dip is very runny, uncover for the last 30 minutes of the cooking time.)

TANGY TOMATO SAUCE

A MORE CONCENTRATED SAUCE CAN BE MADE BY REDUCING THE AMOUNT OF WINE OR STOCK. THERE IS NO DANGER OF THE POT BOILING DRY WHEN YOU USE THE SLOW COOKER TO MAKE SAUCES OR STOCKS.

MAKES	PREPARATION TIME	COOKING TIME	AUTO COOK
750 ml/1¼ pt	10 minutes	Cook on high 3 to 5 hours	5 to 8 hours

1 tbsp sunflower oil

1 onion, peeled and chopped

2–4 garlic cloves, peeled and crushed

1–2 serrano chillies, deseeded and chopped

450 g/1 lb chopped and deseeded ripe tomatoes

2 tbsp tomato purée

2 tsp Worcestershire sauce

450 ml/¾ pt red wine or stock

1 tsp brown sugar

Salt and freshly ground black pepper

1 tsp mixed dried herbs

Preheat the cooker on high. Heat the oil in a frying pan and sauté the onion, garlic and chillies for 3 minutes, then place in the cooking pot. Add all the remaining ingredients and stir well. Cover with the lid and cook on low for 4 hours. Stir well. If a smoother sauce is preferred, blend, then pass through a sieve. Use as directed in recipes.

CREAMY MUSHROOM SAUCE

THIS SAUCE WILL BE PERFECT TO SERVE WITH POACHED CHICKEN OR FISH; ALTERNATIVELY, USE AS THE BASIS FOR A PASTA DISH SUCH AS LASAGNE OR CANNELLONI.

MAKES	PREPARATION TIME	COOKING TIME	AUTO COOK
750 ml/1¼ pt	15 minutes	Cook on low 4 to 6 hours	6 to 9 hours

25 g/1 oz unsalted butter

2 large shallots, peeled and chopped

1 serrano chilli, deseeded and chopped

2–4 garlic cloves, peeled and crushed

450 g/1 lb mushrooms, wiped and finely chopped

450 ml/¾ pt vegetable stock

2 tbsp cornflour

Salt and freshly ground black pepper

3–4 tbsp single cream

Preheat the cooker on high. Melt the butter in a large pan and sauté the shallots, chilli and garlic for 3 minutes. Add the mushrooms and continue to sauté for 3 more minutes. Spoon into the cooking pot and pour over the vegetable stock. Blend the cornflour with 2 tablespoons of water and stir into the pot. Add the seasoning. Cover and cook on low for 4 hours. Adjust seasoning, stir in the cream and use as required, reheating if necessary.

RED WINE SAUCE

REMEMBER, THE 6 HOURS REFERS TO THE ACTUAL COOKING TIME; THE EXTRA 2 HOURS MEAN THAT THE SAUCE WILL HOLD FOR A FURTHER 2 HOURS.

MAKES	PREPARATION TIME	COOKING TIME
600 ml/1 pt	15 minutes	Cook on low 6 to 8 hours

25 g/1 oz unsalted butter

4 shallots, peeled and finely chopped

2 garlic cloves, peeled and crushed

50 g/2 oz mushrooms, wiped and finely chopped

3 tbsp flour

300 ml/½ pt red wine

250 ml/8 fl oz stock

1 tsp redcurrant jelly or clear honey

Salt and freshly ground black pepper

1 Preheat the cooker on high while preparing ingredients. Heat the butter in a pan and sauté the shallots, garlic and mushrooms for 3 minutes. Sprinkle in the flour and cook, stirring, for 1 minute, then take off the heat. Gradually stir in the red wine and then the stock.

2 Add the redcurrant jelly or honey and a little seasoning. Return to the heat and cook, stirring. When the mixture comes to the boil, pour into the cooking pot and cover with the lid. Cook on low for 6 to 8 hours, adjust seasoning and either serve as it is or strain, then serve.

POTATO SOUP WITH CORIANDER

IF PREFERRED, THIS SOUP COULD BE SERVED SLIGHTLY CHUNKY – INSTEAD OF PASSING THROUGH A FOOD PROCESSOR, SIMPLY MASH THE COOKED INGREDIENTS WITH A POTATO MASHER.

SERVES	PREPARATION TIME	COOKING TIME	AUTO COOK
4	25 minutes	Cook on low 5 to 6 hours	6 to 9 hours

25 g/1 oz unsalted butter

4 shallots, peeled and chopped

2–3 garlic cloves, peeled and chopped

450 g/1 lb potatoes, peeled and chopped

2 carrots, peeled and chopped

1 small Bramley cooking apple, peeled, cored and chopped

Grated rind and juice of 1 lemon, preferably unwaxed or organic

1 tsp ground cumin

1 tsp ground coriander

Few strands of saffron

1 tbsp flour

750 ml/1¼ pt vegetable stock

Salt and freshly ground black pepper

1 tbsp fresh coriander, chopped

4 tbsp soured cream

2–4 spring onions, trimmed and finely chopped

1 Preheat the cooker on high. Melt the butter in a large pan and sauté the shallots, garlic, potatoes, carrots and apple for 5 minutes or until slightly softened.

2 Add the lemon rind with the spices, including the saffron, then the flour and cook, stirring, for 2 minutes. Remove from the heat and gradually stir in the stock followed by the lemon juice. Add a little seasoning, then return to the heat and bring to the boil. Spoon or pour into the cooking pot and cover with the lid.

3 Reduce the temperature to low and cook for 5 to 6 hours. Blend until smooth, then stir in the chopped coriander and adjust the seasoning. Reheat if necessary and serve with the soured cream sprinkled with the chopped spring onions.

2

FISH AND SEAFOOD

SALMON WITH SWEET CHILLI GLAZE

THIS RECIPE WILL QUICKLY BECOME A FIRM FAVOURITE. THE SWEET CHILLI GLAZE REALLY BRINGS OUT THE DELICATE FLAVOURS OF THE SALMON. TRY IT FOR YOURSELF AND YOU'LL SEE WHY.

SERVES	PREPARATION TIME	COOKING TIME	AUTO COOK
4	5 minutes	Cook on low 2 to 3 hours	2 hours

4 salmon steaks

1 serrano chilli, deseeded and chopped

1 garlic clove, peeled and crushed

2 tbsp dark brown sugar

1 tbsp light soy sauce

2 tsp lime rind

2 tbsp lime juice

2–3 tsp sweet chilli sauce

1 tbsp honey, optional

Fresh coriander sprigs and lime
  wedges, to garnish

Cooked white and wild rice, to serve

Preheat the slow cooker on high while preparing the ingredients. Lightly rinse the salmon and place in the cooking pot. Blend the remaining ingredients except for the honey and garnishes and pour over the salmon steaks. Cover with the lid, reduce the temperature to low and cook for 2 to 3 hours. If a slightly stickier glaze is preferred, pour the cooking liquor into a small pan, add the honey and boil vigorously for 3 minutes, then pour over the salmon. Garnish and serve with cooked rice.

MONKFISH WITH FENNEL

THE FIRM, WHITE FLESH OF MONKFISH IS SO MEATY THAT IT IS ONE OF THE FEW FISH THAT CAN BE ROASTED WITHOUT ANY DANGER OF SPOILING.

SERVES	PREPARATION TIME	COOKING TIME	AUTO COOK
4	15 minutes	Cook on low 3 to 4 hours	3 to 4 hours

675 g/1½ lb monkfish, central
  bone removed

1 fennel bulb, trimmed and cut
  into wedges

1 red onion, peeled and cut into wedges

1 orange pepper, deseeded and
  cut into wedges

1 red pepper, deseeded and
  cut into wedges

1 tbsp Thai plum sauce

2 tbsp light soy sauce

8 tbsp orange juice

2 tsp honey

½ tsp Thai 7 spice seasoning

Fennel fronds or fresh herbs, to garnish

Cooked rice mixed with chopped fresh
  coriander, to serve

1 Preheat the slow cooker on high while preparing the ingredients. Lightly rinse the fish, pat dry, then cut into bite-sized pieces and reserve. Arrange the fennel, onion and pepper wedges in the base of the cooking pot, then place the fish on top.

2 Blend the remaining ingredients together and pour over the fish and vegetables. Cover with the lid, reduce the temperature to low and cook for 3 to 4 hours. Serve garnished with fennel fronds or fresh herbs accompanied by coriander-flavoured rice.

▶ Salmon with Sweet Chilli Glaze

TROUT WITH PEPPERS

PEPPERS ARE SO EASY TO SKIN. CUT IN HALF, THEN PLACE SKIN-SIDE UP UNDER A PREHEATED GRILL AND COOK UNTIL THE SKINS ARE CHARRED. REMOVE AND PLACE IN A PAPER BAG FOR 10 MINUTES, THEN SKIN.

SERVES	PREPARATION TIME	COOKING TIME	AUTO COOK
4	25 minutes	Cook on low 2 to 3 hours	2 hours

1 tsp unsalted butter

8 small trout fillets

Salt and freshly ground black pepper

¼–½ tsp dried crushed chillies

1 red pepper, skinned and sliced

1 yellow pepper, skinned and sliced

1 shallot, peeled and sliced

1 small orange, sliced

150 ml/¼ pt white wine and water mixed together

1 tbsp toasted flaked almonds

Fresh snipped chives, to garnish, optional

Lemon-flavoured mayonnaise or Hollandaise sauce and freshly cooked vegetables or salad, to serve

1 Preheat the slow cooker on high and smear the inside of the cooking pot with the butter. Skin the fillets, then check that all the bones have been removed, especially the very fine pin bones. Rinse lightly and pat dry with kitchen paper.

2 Place the fillets skinned side down and season lightly with salt and pepper, then sprinkle with a little crushed chilli. Place 2 to 3 strips of each pepper on top of each fillet, then roll up and secure with cocktail sticks.

3 Place the shallot and orange in the base of the cooking pot and place the stuffed fillets on top. Pour over the wine and water. Cover, reduce the temperature to low and cook for 2 to 3 hours. Remove the cocktail sticks, scatter with the almonds and garnish with the snipped chives, if using. Serve with lemon-flavoured mayonnaise or Hollandaise sauce and freshly cooked vegetables or salad.

SPICY SWORDFISH WITH COCONUT

THIS RECIPE WILL WORK EQUALLY WELL WITH SALMON, TUNA OR ANY OTHER FRESH FISH FILLETS. SMOKED FISH, HOWEVER, WOULD NOT COMBINE WELL WITH THE FLAVOURS USED.

SERVES	PREPARATION TIME	COOKING TIME	AUTO COOK
4	15 minutes	Cook on low 2 to 3 hours	2 hours

1 tbsp sunflower oil

1 tsp cumin seeds

1 red serrano chilli, deseeded and chopped

1 garlic clove, peeled and crushed

1 lemon grass stalk, outer leaves discarded and chopped

1 tbsp grated lime rind

2 tbsp light soy sauce

1 tsp Thai fish sauce

150 ml/¼ pt coconut milk

4 swordfish steaks

1 tbsp chopped fresh coriander

Cooked sticky jasmine rice and an Asian-style salad

1 Preheat the slow cooker on high while preparing the ingredients. Heat the oil in a frying pan and gently fry the cumin seeds, chilli, garlic and lemon grass for 3 minutes, then drain on kitchen paper. Blend with the grated lime rind, soy and fish sauces and the coconut milk and reserve.

2 Lightly rinse the swordfish and place in the cooking pot. Pour over the coconut milk mixture and cover with the lid.

3 Reduce the temperature to low and cook for 2 to 3 hours. Serve sprinkled with the chopped coriander accompanied by sticky jasmine rice and an Asian-style salad.

FISH PROVENÇAL

WHEN COOKING FISH IN THE SLOW COOKER IT IS BEST TO SKIN IT FIRST. SLIP A LONG SHARP KNIFE UNDER THE SKIN AT THE TAIL END, THEN SLIP IT DOWN THE LENGTH OF THE FISH OR, IF THE FISH IS FIRM FLESHED, RIP THE SKIN OFF.

SERVES	PREPARATION TIME	COOKING TIME	AUTO COOK
4	10 minutes	Cook on low 3 to 4 hours	3 to 4 hours

4 cod or other firm white fish fillets
    about 550 g/1¼ lb

1 onion, peeled and sliced

1 yellow pepper, deseeded and sliced

425-g/15-oz can artichoke hearts,
    drained and cut in half

4 firm tomatoes, sliced

50 g/2 oz pitted black olives

1 bay leaf

Salt and freshly ground black pepper

120 ml/4 fl oz medium dry white wine

Snipped fresh chives, to garnish

Warm crusty bread or new potatoes
    and salad, to serve

1 Preheat the slow cooker on high. Skin the fish if necessary, cut into bite-sized pieces and place in the cooking pot. Add the remaining ingredients except for the wine and chives. Bring the wine to just below boiling point, pour over the fish, then cover with the lid.

2 Reduce the temperature to low and cook for 3 to 4 hours. Serve garnished with chives and with either warm crusty bread or new potatoes and salad.

FRESH SALMON MOUSSE

CHOP THE FISH REALLY FINELY FOR THIS MOUSSE SO THAT THE FISH IS EVENLY DISTRIBUTED THROUGHOUT. SERVE WITH A TOSSED GREEN SALAD AND MELBA TOAST FOR A DELICIOUS SUMMER LUNCH.

SERVES	PREPARATION TIME	COOKING TIME
6 to 8	20 minutes	Cook on low 5 to 6 hours

50 g/2 oz unsalted butter

50 g/2 oz flour

300 ml/½ pt semi-skimmed milk

150 ml/¼ pt low-fat soured cream

Salt and freshly ground black pepper

½ tsp freshly grated nutmeg

1 tbsp chopped fresh chervil

225 g/8 oz cod fillet, skinned and boned

450 g/1 lb fresh salmon fillet, skinned
    and boned

Grated rind and juice of 1 lemon

2 medium eggs, beaten

Chervil sprigs and lemon wedges,
    to garnish

Melba toast, to serve

1 Preheat the slow cooker on high. Lightly butter a 1.2-litre/2-pint heatproof dish and reserve. Melt the butter in a pan and sprinkle in the flour. Cook, stirring, for 2 minutes, then take off the heat and stir in the milk. Return to the heat and cook, stirring, until thickened. Remove from the heat and stir in the soured cream with seasoning, nutmeg and chervil.

2 Finely chop the cod and salmon by hand or in the food processor, then stir into the prepared sauce. Add the lemon rind and juice. Pour in the beaten eggs and lightly stir the mixture until it is well mixed. Spoon into the buttered dish and smooth the top. Cover with lightly buttered tinfoil and place in the cooking pot. Pour in sufficient water to come almost to the top of the pot, cover, reduce temperature to low and cook for 5 to 6 hours. Remove, allow to cool, then chill until required. Garnish and serve with Melba toast.

SOLE WITH BACON AND APRICOTS

THIS RECIPE WORKS BEST WITH LARGE FILLETS, WHICH ARE EASIER TO STUFF, BUT OF COURSE IT IS ALWAYS A MATTER OF PERSONAL TASTE.

SERVES	PREPARATION TIME	COOKING TIME	AUTO COOK
4	15 minutes	Cook on low 2 to 3 hours	3 to 5 hours

4 large or 8 small sole fillets, skinned

Salt and freshly ground black pepper

4 rashers bacon

12–16 ready-to-eat dried apricots

1 tbsp cornflour

250 ml/8 fl oz orange juice

1–2 tsp maple syrup

Lime wedges, to garnish

Creamed potatoes mixed with spring onions and cooked vegetables, to serve

1 Preheat the cooker on high. Place the fillets skinned side down onto a chopping board and season lightly. Remove any excess fat from the bacon, then place on top of the fish. If using 8 small fillets, cut the bacon in half lengthways. Cut the apricots into 3 pieces and place on top of the bacon. Roll up, starting from the tail end. Secure with cocktail sticks if necessary. Place in the cooking pot.

2 Blend the cornflour with the orange juice and maple syrup, bring to the boil, stirring, and pour over the sole fillets. Cover with the lid and cook on low for 2 to 3 hours. Remove from the pot, pour around the orange sauce and serve garnished with lime wedges accompanied by creamed potatoes and vegetables.

FISH AND PRAWN PAELLA

DO MAKE SURE THAT THE PEAS, SWEETCORN AND PRAWNS ARE THOROUGHLY THAWED BEFORE ADDING TO THE PAELLA.

SERVES	PREPARATION TIME	COOKING TIME	AUTO COOK
6	20 minutes	Cook on low 3 to 4 hours	2 hours

1 tbsp sunflower oil

1 medium onion, peeled and chopped

2–4 garlic cloves, peeled and crushed

½–1 tsp dried crushed chillies

450 g/1 lb monkfish, cubed

Pinch saffron powder

185 g/6 oz easy-cook long-grain rice

600 ml/1 pt fish or vegetable stock

1 red pepper, deseeded and chopped

1 yellow pepper, deseeded and chopped

3 tomatoes, deseeded and chopped

Salt and freshly ground black pepper

75 g/3 oz thawed frozen peas

50 g/2 oz thawed frozen sweetcorn kernels

175 g/6 oz peeled prawns, thawed if frozen

Few cooked mussels in their shells, whole cooked prawns, lemon wedges and 2 tbsp chopped fresh coriander, to garnish

1 Preheat the slow cooker on high. Heat the oil in a frying pan and sauté the onion, garlic and chillies for 3 minutes. Add the monkfish, saffron powder and rice and stir well. Pour in the stock followed by the chopped peppers, tomatoes and a little seasoning. Bring to the boil. Transfer to the cooking pot and cover with the lid.

2 Reduce the temperature to low and cook for 3 to 4 hours. One hour before the end of the cooking time add the peas, sweetcorn and prawns and continue to cook. Serve garnished with the mussels, prawns, lemon wedges and chopped coriander.

◀ Sole with Bacon and Apricots

SKATE WITH TOMATOES AND OLIVES

THE FLAVOUR OF ANY FISH COOKED IN THE SLOW COOKER IS SUPERB. THIS IS ESPECIALLY TRUE WITH DELICATE-TASTING FISH SUCH AS SKATE.

SERVES	PREPARATION TIME	COOKING TIME	AUTO COOK
4	15 minutes	Cook on low 2 to 4 hours	2 hours

4 small skate wings

2–3 tbsp flour

Salt and freshly ground black pepper

1 tbsp unsalted butter

550 g/1¼ lb new potatoes, scrubbed and thickly sliced

1 medium onion, peeled and sliced

3 medium tomatoes, peeled, deseeded and chopped

1 orange pepper, deseeded and sliced

50 g/2 oz stuffed green olives

1–2 tbsp capers, drained

120 ml/4 fl oz white wine or orange juice

1 tbsp chopped fresh basil and basil sprigs, to serve

Preheat the slow cooker on high. Rinse the skate wings and dip in the flour seasoned with salt and pepper. Heat the butter and brush a little around the cooking pot. Put the potatoes in the base of the pot, topped with the skate wings. Gently sauté the onion in the remaining butter for 3 minutes then add the remaining ingredients, except the basil and season to taste. Pour over the skate wings, cover with the lid, reduce the temperature to low and cook for 2 to 4 hours. Sprinkle with the basil and serve.

FISH AND PASTA BAKE

DRIED PASTA WILL GIVE FAR BETTER RESULTS WHEN COOKED IN THE SLOW COOKER. DO NOT USE REFRIGERATED PASTA AS THIS WILL BECOME SOGGY.

SERVES	PREPARATION TIME	COOKING TIME	AUTO COOK
4	15 minutes	Cook on low 3 to 4 hours	3 to 4 hours

1 tbsp unsalted butter

1 medium onion, peeled and chopped

1 small red jalapeño chilli, deseeded and chopped

100 g/4 oz chopped button mushrooms

450 g/1 lb fresh tuna steak, skinned and cut into cubes

1 ripe mango, peeled, stoned and chopped

3 tomatoes, deseeded and chopped

100 g/4 oz dried pasta shapes

600 ml/1 pt mango or orange juice

Salt and freshly ground black pepper

2 tbsp chopped fresh coriander, to garnish

Strips of warm pitta bread, to serve

Preheat the slow cooker on high. Heat the butter in a frying pan and sauté the onion and chilli for 3 minutes. Add the mushrooms and cook for another minute. Stir in the remaining ingredients except for the coriander and transfer to the cooking pot. Cover with the lid, reduce the temperature to low and cook for 3 to 4 hours. Serve sprinkled with the coriander and with pitta bread.

SCALLOP, PRAWN AND SAFFRON RICE

IT IS PREFERABLE TO USE SAFFRON STRANDS RATHER THAN SAFFRON POWDER. EITHER SOAK THE STRANDS IN WARM WATER FOR A FEW MINUTES, THEN USE BOTH THE STRANDS AND SOAKING LIQUOR, OR SPRINKLE STRAIGHT INTO THE DISH AT THE BEGINNING OF COOKING.

SERVES	PREPARATION TIME	COOKING TIME
4	10 minutes	Cook on low 2 to 3 hours

2 tbsp unsalted butter

1 onion, peeled and chopped

2 medium leeks, trimmed and sliced

Few saffron strands

175 g/6 oz easy-cook brown long-grain rice, rinsed

300 g/10 oz scallops, rinsed and halved if large

225 g/8 oz large uncooked, peeled prawns

600 ml/1 pt fish or chicken stock

1 orange pepper, peeled and chopped

4 tomatoes, deseeded and chopped

Salt and freshly ground black pepper

2 tbsp chopped fresh parsley

2 medium eggs, hard-boiled, shelled and quartered, to garnish

1 Preheat the cooker on high. Wipe the cooking pot with a little of the butter, then heat the remaining butter in the frying pan and sauté the onion and leeks for 3 minutes, stirring frequently. Add the saffron and rice and continue to sauté for 2 minutes. Add the scallops and prawns and cook for 3 minutes, stirring, then add the remaining ingredients except for the parsley and eggs and bring to the boil.

2 Spoon into the cooking pot, cover with the lid and cook for 2 to 3 hours. Stir, adjust the seasoning, then serve immediately sprinkled with the parsley and garnished with the hard-boiled eggs.

CHEESE AND PRAWN FONDUE

THIS DISH IS IDEAL FOR LONG HOT SUMMER DAYS WHEN YOU DO NOT FEEL LIKE COOKING. THE BEAUTY OF USING THE SLOW COOKER IN THE SUMMER IS THAT IT DOES NOT HEAT THE KITCHEN.

SERVES	PREPARATION TIME	COOKING TIME
6 to 8	15 minutes	Cook on low 1 to 3 hours

1 tbsp unsalted butter

2 shallots, peeled and finely chopped

175 g/6 oz large raw prawns, peeled

1 garlic clove, peeled

350 g/12 oz Gruyère or Swiss cheese, grated

2 tsp cornflour

150 ml/¼ pt beer or light ale

Few drops hot pepper sauce

Fresh chopped parsley, to garnish

Vegetable crudités, cubes of French bread and pretzels, as dippers

1 Preheat the cooker on high while preparing the ingredients. Heat the butter in a small pan until melted, then sauté the chopped shallots for 3 minutes. Rinse the prawns and dry on kitchen paper, then add to the shallots and cook for 3 more minutes. Remove from the pan, drain on kitchen paper and reserve.

2 Rub the inside of the cooking pot with the peeled garlic clove, then place the grated cheese into the pot. Blend the cornflour with the beer and hot pepper sauce and pour into the pot, stir, then cover with the lid. Cook on low for 1 hour, or until the cheese has melted. Stir in the reserved cooked shallots and prawns and either use immediately or keep for 2 hours. Sprinkle with chopped parsley and serve with the vegetable crudités, cubes of French bread and pretzels.

DOVER SOLE WITH LEMON AND CHIVE BUTTER

COOKING FISH IN THE SLOW COOKER HAS TWO MAIN ADVANTAGES: THE DELICATE FLAVOURS OF THE FISH ARE INTENSIFIED AND THE NUTRITIONAL VALUES ARE PRESERVED.

SERVES	PREPARATION TIME	COOKING TIME	AUTO COOK
4	10 minutes	Cook on low 2 to 3 hours	3 to 4 hours

50 g/2 oz softened butter

4 Dover or lemon sole, filleted and skinned

Salt and freshly ground black pepper

Grated rind from 1 lemon

Small bunch chives, snipped

3 tbsp lemon juice

Lemon wedges and fresh chives, to garnish

Salad or freshly cooked vegetables and new potatoes, to serve

1 Preheat the cooker on high. Smear the cooking pot with a little of the butter. Lightly rinse and pat dry the fish fillets and place skinned side down on a chopping board. Season with salt and pepper, then sprinkle with a little grated lemon rind. Sprinkle each fillet with a few snipped chives, then roll up, starting from the head end. Place in the cooking pot.

2 Pour the lemon juice around the fish. Dot with the remaining butter, cover and cook on low for 2 to 3 hours. Carefully remove from the pot and pour over the chive butter sauce that has formed in the pot. Garnish with lemon wedges and chives accompanied by salad or vegetables and new potatoes.

TUNA WITH MANGO SALSA

THIS RECIPE, USING A MANGO SALSA, WOULD WORK WELL WITH SWORDFISH OR SALMON. BEAT THE REFRIED BEANS SO THAT THEY ARE NOT TOO LUMPY.

SERVES	PREPARATION TIME	COOKING TIME	AUTO COOK
4	15 minutes	Cook on low 3 to 4 hours	4 to 6 hours

1 tsp sunflower oil

3 tbsp white wine

425-g/15-oz can refried beans

4 tuna steaks, each about 150 g/5 oz

Salt and freshly ground black pepper

1 small ripe mango, peeled, stoned and finely chopped

4 shallots, peeled and finely chopped

1–2 green jalapeño chillies, deseeded and chopped

1–2 garlic cloves, peeled and crushed

3 ripe but firm tomatoes, deseeded and chopped

2 tbsp chopped fresh coriander

Flat leaf parsley sprigs, to garnish

Cooked rice and salad, to serve

1   Preheat the cooker on high. Lightly oil the cooking pot with the sunflower oil. Place the wine and beans into the cooking pot and heat through while preparing the remaining ingredients. Lightly rinse the tuna steaks, pat dry, season and reserve. Stir together the mango, shallots, chillies, garlic, tomatoes and coriander.

2   Beat the refried beans in the cooking pot until smooth, then place the tuna on top of the beans. Spoon over the mango salsa, cover and cook on low for 3 to 4 hours. Garnish with parsley sprigs and serve with freshly cooked rice and a salad.

FISH CREOLE

YOU CAN VARY THE FISH ACCORDING TO AVAILABILITY AND PERSONAL TASTE. CHOOSE A FISH WHOSE FLAVOUR WILL NOT BE LOST IN THE ROBUST SAUCE.

SERVES	PREPARATION TIME	COOKING TIME
4	15 minutes	Cook on low 3 to 4 hours

1 tbsp sunflower oil

1 large onion, peeled and chopped

6 garlic cloves, peeled and crushed

2 celery sticks, trimmed and chopped

2 large tomatoes, deseeded and chopped

1 red pepper, deseeded and finely chopped

2 tbsp tomato purée

450 ml/¾ pt fish or chicken stock

Few dashes hot pepper sauce

1 tbsp lime juice

1 tsp dark brown sugar

1 tsp dried thyme

350 g/12 oz orange roughy fillets, skinned and cut into bite-sized pieces

Salt and freshly ground black pepper

100 g/4 oz peeled prawns, thawed if frozen

1 tbsp chopped fresh thyme, to garnish

Cooked rice, to serve

1   Preheat the cooker on high while preparing the ingredients. Heat the oil in a large pan and sauté the onion, garlic and celery for 3 minutes. Add the tomatoes and red pepper and stir well.

2   Blend the tomato purée with the stock and pour into the pan together with the hot pepper sauce, lime juice, sugar and dried thyme. Bring to the boil, then pour into the cooking pot. Add the fish with a little seasoning, cover with the lid and cook for 2½ hours. Add the prawns and continue to cook for an additional 30 minutes to 1½ hours. Adjust seasoning, then serve sprinkled with the chopped thyme accompanied by the freshly cooked rice.

PLAICE WITH ARTICHOKE AND CAPER DRESSING

SLICE THE POTATOES THINLY AND ENSURE THAT THE LIQUOR COVERS THEM. ROOT VEGETABLES TAKE LONGER TO COOK IN THE SLOW COOKER THAN FISH OR MEAT.

SERVES	PREPARATION TIME	COOKING TIME	AUTO COOK
4	20 minutes	Cook on low 2 to 3 hours	2 hours

4 large or 8 small plaice fillets

1 tbsp unsalted butter

2 small shallots, peeled and chopped

40 g/1½ oz button mushrooms, finely chopped

2 tsp grated lemon rind

40 g/1½ oz soft breadcrumbs

Salt and freshly ground black pepper

1 tbsp chopped fresh tarragon

1 egg yolk, beaten

150 ml/¼ pt orange juice or white wine

450 g/1 lb new potatoes, scrubbed and thinly sliced

425-g/15-oz can artichoke hearts, drained and halved

2 large tomatoes, sliced

2 tbsp capers

Fresh tarragon, to garnish

Green salad, or vegetables, to serve

1 Preheat the slow cooker on high. Skin the plaice fillets if necessary and reserve. Heat the butter in a small pan and sauté the shallots for 2 minutes, then add the mushrooms and continue to sauté for 1 minute. Remove from the heat and stir in the lemon rind, breadcrumbs, seasoning and tarragon. Mix well, then bind together with the egg yolk and a little orange juice or wine, if necessary.

2 Place the fish skinned side down and divide the stuffing between the fillets. Roll up and secure with a cocktail stick. Place the sliced potatoes, artichoke hearts and tomatoes in the base of the cooking pot and scatter with the capers. Place the stuffed fillets on top, then pour over the orange juice or wine. Cover and reduce the heat to low, then cook for 2 to 3 hours. Garnish with tarragon and serve with a green salad or vegetables.

BARBECUED TUNA

CHOOSE ANY FIRM FISH FOR THIS DISH—SWORDFISH OR MONKFISH WOULD WORK WELL. CHOOSE THE FRESHEST-LOOKING FISH AVAILABLE.

SERVES	PREPARATION TIME	COOKING TIME
4	10 minutes	Cook on low 3 to 4 hours

1 green pepper, deseeded and chopped

1 onion, peeled and finely chopped

1–2 garlic cloves, peeled and crushed

½–1 tsp dried crushed chillies

1 tbsp Worcestershire sauce

2 tbsp dark sugar

3 tbsp wine vinegar

2 tsp American mustard

150 ml/¼ pt tomato juice

Hot pepper sauce, to taste

4 tuna steaks, each about 150 g/5 oz

Fresh coriander sprigs, to garnish

Preheat the cooker on high. Blend all the ingredients together except for the fish and herbs in a pan and bring to the boil. Remove from the heat and stir until blended. Lightly rinse the fish steaks, then place in the cooking pot. Pour over the barbecue sauce and cover with the lid. Cook for 3 to 4 hours, then serve with the sauce garnished with the fresh coriander sprigs.

CHAPTER THREE

MEAT

BOEUF BOURGUIGNON

THE SLOW COOKER COOKS THIS CLASSIC FRENCH DISH SO THAT IT SIMPLY MELTS IN THE MOUTH. TRY IT WITH THE CREAMY MASHED POTATOES FLAVOURED WITH SPRING ONIONS TO BRING THE RECIPE RIGHT UP TO DATE.

SERVES	PREPARATION TIME	COOKING TIME	AUTO COOK
4	25 minutes plus overnight marinating time	Cook on low 5 to 7 hours	7 to 10 hours

675 g/1½ lb braising steak or topside

300 ml/½ pt red wine

2 tbsp brandy

2 tbsp sunflower oil

175 g/6 oz piece gammon, rind and fat removed, and diced small

8–12 baby onions, peeled

4–6 garlic cloves, peeled but left whole

3 tbsp flour

150 ml/¼ pt beef stock

Few fresh thyme sprigs

Creamy mashed potatoes flavoured with spring onion, to serve

Fresh thyme sprigs, to garnish

1 Preheat the slow cooker on high while preparing ingredients. (If marinating overnight, heat just before cooking.) Trim and discard any fat or gristle from the beef and cut into cubes. Place in a shallow dish and pour over the red wine and brandy. Cover and leave to marinate for at least 30 minutes, or overnight if time permits. When ready to cook, drain, reserving the marinade.

2 Heat the oil in a large pan and sear the beef and chopped bacon on all sides, remove and reserve. Add the whole baby onions and garlic and sauté for 5 minutes, stirring frequently. Then return the seared meat to the pan. Sprinkle in the flour and cook, stirring, for 3 minutes, then take off the heat. Gradually stir in the reserved marinade and the stock.

3 Bring to the boil, then transfer to the cooking pot and add the thyme sprigs. Cover, reduce the heat and cook for 5 to 7 hours. Adjust seasoning and serve with the spring onion-flavoured mashed potatoes.

BEEF AND HORSERADISH SANDWICH

WHEN COOKING WHOLE JOINTS, CHECK THAT THE JOINT WILL FIT IN THE SLOW COOKING POT AND THAT THE LID FITS PROPERLY, OTHERWISE, THE COOKER WILL NOT WORK EFFICIENTLY.

SERVES	PREPARATION TIME	COOKING TIME
4 to 6	5 minutes	Cook on high 3 to 5 hours

900-g/2-lb beef joint such as topside

1 tbsp creamed horseradish sauce

1 tbsp Worcestershire sauce

3 tbsp tomato ketchup

1 tbsp balsamic vinegar

2 tbsp maple syrup

Large warm rolls, rocket, sliced red onion, sliced large tomatoes, grated Monterey Jack or strong Cheddar cheese with assorted relishes and pickles, to serve

1 Preheat the slow cooker on high. Wipe the joint and place in the slow cooker cooking pot. Blend the horseradish and Worcestershire sauce with the tomato ketchup, balsamic vinegar, maple syrup and 4 tablespoons of water, then pour over the joint. Cover and cook on high for 3 to 5 hours.

2 Remove and allow to cool slightly before slicing and serving on rolls with the rocket, sliced red onion, sliced tomatoes, grated cheese and assorted relishes and pickles.

CHILLI CON CARNE

IF PREFERRED, YOU CAN USE BRAISING STEAK CUT INTO SMALL PIECES IN PLACE OF THE MINCED BEEF.

SERVES	PREPARATION TIME	COOKING TIME	AUTO COOK
4	25 minutes	Cook on low 8 to 10 hours	9 to 12 hours

450 g/1 lb minced beef

1 tsp sunflower oil

1 medium onion, peeled and chopped

2–3 red jalapeño chillies, deseeded and chopped

2–4 garlic cloves, peeled and crushed

2 celery sticks, trimmed and finely chopped

450 g/1 lb ripe tomatoes, peeled and chopped

2 tbsp tomato purée

2 tbsp chopped fresh coriander

Salt and freshly ground black pepper

410-g/14½-oz can red kidney beans, drained and rinsed

100 g/4 oz sweetcorn kernels, thawed if frozen

Cooked rice, grated Monterey Jack cheese, soured cream, hot chilli sauce, pickled jalapeño chillies and tortilla chips, to serve

1 Preheat the slow cooker on high. Place the minced beef in a frying pan and heat gently, stirring frequently, until the beef is seared and any fat has run out. Drain the beef through a strainer and reserve. Wipe the pan clean.

2 Heat the oil in the cleaned frying pan and sauté the onion, chillies, garlic and celery for 5 minutes or until beginning to soften. Return the minced beef to the pan, then stir in the chopped tomatoes.

3 Blend the tomato purée with 6 tablespoons of water, then stir into the beef mixture with 1 tablespoon of the chopped coriander, seasoning and the red kidney beans.

4 Pour into the cooking pot, cover and reduce the temperature to low. Cook for 7 to 9 hours, then stir in the sweetcorn and continue to cook for 1 hour.

5 Adjust the seasoning. Serve with rice, cheese, soured cream, hot chilli sauce, pickled chillies and tortilla chips.

CHILLI TACOS

THIS FILLING WOULD ALSO BE GREAT IF USED TO MAKE ENCHILADAS OR TOSTADAS. MAKE A DOUBLE BATCH AND FREEZE HALF FOR LATER.

SERVES	PREPARATION TIME	COOKING TIME	AUTO COOK
6	15 minutes	Cook on low 3 to 4 hours	4 to 6 hours

450 g/1 lb minced beef

1 tbsp sunflower oil

1 large onion, peeled and finely chopped

2–4 garlic cloves, peeled and crushed

2 celery sticks, trimmed and chopped

1–2 tsp hot chilli powder, to taste

$\frac{1}{2}$ tsp ground cinnamon

$\frac{1}{2}$ tsp ground coriander

$\frac{1}{2}$ tsp ground cloves

1 green pepper, deseeded and finely chopped

410-g/14$\frac{1}{2}$-oz can chopped tomatoes

200 g/7 oz canned red kidney beans or chick peas, drained and rinsed

100 g/4 oz pickled chillies, drained and chopped

150 ml/$\frac{1}{4}$ pt beef stock

Salt and freshly ground black pepper

1 tbsp fresh chopped coriander

1 small avocado, peeled, stoned and sliced

Soured cream, lime wedges and taco shells, to serve

1 Preheat cooker on high while preparing ingredients. Heat a large frying pan and fry the beef, stirring frequently, to break up any lumps, until seared. Remove from the heat and reserve.

2 Add the oil to the pan and sauté the onion, garlic and celery for 3 minutes. Add the chilli powder and spices and fry for another 2 minutes, stirring frequently. Return the beef to the pan, stir, then add the remaining ingredients except for the chopped coriander and avocado. Bring to the boil, then pour into the cooking pot.

3 Cover with the lid and cook on low for 3 to 4 hours. Serve sprinkled with the chopped coriander, sliced avocado, lime wedges, soured cream and taco shells. If the chilli mixture is too wet, remove the lid at the end of the cooking time, turn the heat up to high and cook uncovered for 20 to 30 minutes.

BLACK BEANS WITH SAUSAGE

THIS IS A HEARTY DISH AND IS GREAT WHEN SERVED WITH PLENTY OF FRESHLY GRATED HARD CHEESE, SUCH AS MONTEREY JACK OR CHEDDAR, WARM CRUSTY BREAD AND A TOSSED GREEN SALAD.

SERVES	PREPARATION TIME	COOKING TIME	AUTO COOK
4 to 6	10 minutes plus overnight soaking	Cook on high 6 to 8 hours	8 to 10 hours

225 g/8 oz dried black beans, soaked overnight

1 tbsp sunflower oil

1 large red onion, peeled and chopped

2–4 garlic cloves, peeled and crushed

2 celery sticks, trimmed and chopped

½–1 tsp dried crushed chillies

1 tsp ground cumin

1 tsp dried mustard powder

1 green pepper, deseeded and chopped

8 spicy pork or Toulouse sausages

410-g/14½-oz can chopped tomatoes

1 tbsp maple syrup

300 ml/½ pt beef or chicken stock

2 fresh bay leaves

Salt and freshly ground black pepper

1 tbsp chopped fresh thyme, to garnish

1 Soak the black beans overnight in plenty of cold water. Next day, preheat the cooker on high while preparing the ingredients. Drain the beans, rinse and place in a large pan, cover with cold water and bring to the boil. Boil steadily for 10 minutes, then drain and place in the cooking pot. Meanwhile, heat the oil in a large frying pan and sauté the onion, garlic and celery with the chillies, cumin and mustard powder for 3 minutes. Add the pepper, stir well, spoon into the cooker and stir into the beans.

2 Add the sausages to the pan and cook until browned all over. Remove and place on top of the bean mixture. Blend the tomatoes with the maple syrup and stock, then pour over the sausages and add the bay leaves to the pot. Cover and cook on high for 6 to 8 hours. Add seasoning to taste, sprinkle with the chopped thyme and serve.

PORK CASSOULET

THIS CASSOULET IS IDEAL FOR HEARTY APPETITES. SERVE WITH PLENTY OF CORNBREAD AND A TOSSED GREEN SALAD FOR A SATISFYING AND FILLING MEAL.

SERVES	PREPARATION TIME	COOKING TIME	AUTO COOK
4	20 minutes	Cook on low 6 to 8 hours	10 to 12 hours

300 g/10 oz belly of pork, cubed

8 thick Toulouse or pork sausages

1 medium onion, peeled and chopped

3–4 garlic cloves, peeled and chopped

3 celery sticks, trimmed and chopped

1 tbsp freshly chopped marjoram

1 tbsp freshly chopped thyme

Salt and freshly ground black pepper

300 g/10 oz canned cannellini beans, drained and rinsed

300 g/10 oz canned black eye peas, drained and rinsed

410-g/14½-oz can chopped tomatoes

50 g/2 oz soft breadcrumbs

Fresh herbs, to garnish

1 Preheat the slow cooker on high. Place the pork in a frying pan and heat gently until the fat begins to run out. Prick the sausages and add to the pan and brown all over. Remove and chop into large chunks. Add the onion, garlic and celery to the pan, cook for 3 minutes, then add the chopped herbs with seasoning.

2 Layer the pork and onion mixture with the beans, peas and chopped sausages in the cooking pot, then pour over the chopped tomatoes with their juice. Sprinkle over the breadcrumbs and cover with the lid.

3 Reduce the temperature to low and cook for 6 to 8 hours. Serve garnished with fresh herbs.

FRUITY PORK CHOPS

YOU WILL FIND THAT COOKING MEAT IN THE SLOW COOKER PREVENTS THE MEAT FROM SHRINKING AS MUCH AS IT DOES WHEN COOKED CONVENTIONALLY.

SERVES	PREPARATION TIME	COOKING TIME	AUTO COOK
4	15 minutes	Cook on low 4 to 6 hours	6 to 8 hours

4 boneless pork chops

2 carrots, peeled and cut into slices

1 medium onion, peeled and sliced

1 red pepper, deseeded and sliced

75 g/3 oz ready-to-eat dried apricots

1 tbsp brown sugar

1 tbsp tomato purée

1 tsp ground cinnamon

1 tsp hot chilli sauce, or to taste

1 tbsp red wine vinegar

1 tbsp grated orange rind

300 ml/½ pt mango or
    orange juice

Salt and freshly ground black pepper

1½ tbsp cornflour

1 large ripe mango, stoned, peeled
    and diced

175 g/6 oz roughly diced courgette

Warm bread or cooked rice, to serve

Lime wedges and watercress,
    to garnish

1 Preheat the slow cooker on high. Trim off any excess fat from the chops and place in the cooking pot. Scatter over the sliced carrots, onion, pepper and dried apricots. Blend together the brown sugar, the tomato purée, ground cinnamon and hot chilli sauce, then stir in the vinegar and orange rind.

2 Blend the mango or orange juice into the sugar mixture then pour over the pork chops. Add a little seasoning. Cover with a lid and reduce the temperature to low and cook for 3 to 5 hours.

3 Blend the cornflour with 2 tablespoons of water, then stir into the pot with the diced mango and courgettes and cook for 1 more hour before serving with warm bread or rice, garnished with lime and watercress.

BARBECUED RIBS

THE FLAVOUR OF THESE RIBS IS WONDERFUL. MAKE SURE THAT YOU PROVIDE PLENTY OF NAPKINS – YOU WILL FIND THAT EVERYONE NEEDS THEM!

SERVES	PREPARATION TIME	COOKING TIME	AUTO COOK
4	5 minutes	Cook on high 1 hour then low 3 to 4 hours	8 to 10 hours

1 medium onion, finely chopped

3–4 garlic cloves, peeled and crushed

1 tbsp soft brown sugar

4 tbsp tomato ketchup

2 tbsp maple syrup

1 tsp ready-made mustard

1 tsp horseradish sauce

2 tbsp white wine vinegar

2 tbsp Worcestershire sauce

4 tbsp orange juice

900 g/2 lb pork ribs

Fresh herbs, to garnish

Potato salad, baked beans and savoury
    scones, to serve

1 Preheat the slow cooker on high. Blend all the ingredients except the ribs in a pan and stir until well blended; then bring to just below boiling point. Place the ribs in the cooking pot and pour the almost boiling sauce over the ribs. Cover and cook on high for 1 hour. Reduce the temperature of the slow cooker to low and continue to cook for 3 to 4 hours.

2 Remove and arrange on the serving platter and keep warm. Pour the sauce into a pan and boil vigorously until reduced by half, then pour over the ribs, garnish with fresh herbs and serve with potato salad, baked beans and savoury scones.

AROMATIC PORK

THIS EASY-TO-MAKE RECIPE TAKES ITS INSPIRATION FROM THE WONDERFUL
FRAGRANT FLAVOURS OF THAILAND. SERVE WITH FRESHLY COOKED STICKY RICE
AND A GREEN SALAD.

SERVES	PREPARATION TIME	COOKING TIME	AUTO COOK
4	20 minutes plus 30 minutes marinating time	Cook on low 5 to 7 hours	8 to 10 hours

2 lemon grass stalks

Small piece root ginger, peeled and grated

1–2 serrano chillies, deseeded and chopped

1–2 star anise

2 kaffir lime leaves, chopped, or crumbled if dried

300 ml/½ pt orange juice

2–3 tsp clear honey, or to taste

675 g/1½ lb pork tenderloin (2 whole fillets), trimmed

2 tbsp sunflower oil

4–6 shallots, peeled and cut into wedges

2–3 garlic cloves, peeled and crushed

1 tbsp Thai plum sauce

Fresh coriander sprigs and fresh plums, to garnish

1 Preheat the slow cooker on high. Remove and discard the outer leaves of the lemon grass and chop the inner part finely. Mix together the chopped lemon grass, ginger, chillies, star anise, lime leaves, 150 ml/¼ pint of the orange juice and honey.

2 Cut the pork fillets in half and place in a shallow dish. Rub or brush the marinade over the fillet then cover loosely and leave for at least 30 minutes in the refrigerator.

3 When ready to cook, drain the pork if necessary, reserving the marinade. Heat the oil in a frying pan and seal the pork fillet all over. Remove and place in the cooking pot. Add the shallots and garlic to the frying pan and sauté for 3 minutes. Add the marinade, stir well and cook for 1 minute; then add the remaining juice and Thai plum sauce. Bring to the boil, then pour over the pork fillet and cover with the lid.

4 Reduce the temperature to low and cook for 5 to 7 hours. Serve sliced, garnished with fresh coriander sprigs and fresh plums, if available. If a thicker sauce is preferred, strain off the liquor and heat to almost boiling. Blend 2 teaspoons of cornflour with 1 tablespoon of water and stir into the boiling liquor. Cook until thickened and serve with the pork.

LEMON PORK WITH CUMIN

IF YOU LIKE CRISP SKIN ON THE JOINT, DO NOT BROWN THE JOINT BEFORE
COOKING. ONCE COOKED, REMOVE THE PORK JOINT FROM THE COOKER AND
GRILL THE SKIN UNDER A PREHEATED GRILL FOR ABOUT 10 MINUTES.

SERVES	PREPARATION TIME	COOKING TIME	AUTO COOK
6	20 minutes	Cook on low 5 to 7 hours	8 to 10 hours

1.5 kg/3 lb pork leg joint

1 tbsp unsalted butter

1 medium onion, peeled and chopped

2–4 garlic cloves, peeled and chopped

1 tsp cumin deseeds

1 large lemon, preferably unwaxed or
 organic, cut into wedges

150 ml/¼ pt dry white wine

300 ml/½ pt vegetable or chicken stock

1 tbsp soy sauce

Few fresh sage leaves

1 tbsp cornflour

Lemon wedges and fresh sage
 leaves, to garnish

Freshly cooked vegetables, to serve

1 Preheat the slow cooker on high. Discard the rind and any excess fat
from the pork joint. Heat the butter in a frying pan, sear the pork on all
sides and place in the cooking pot.

2 Add the onion, garlic and cumin to the butter remaining in the frying
pan and sauté for 3 minutes, stirring frequently. Add the lemon
wedges to the pan and continue to sauté for 3 minutes; then spoon
over the pork joint.

3 Blend the wine, stock and soy sauce and pour over the joint; then
add the sage leaves. Cover with a lid, reduce the heat to low and
cook for 5 to 7 hours. Remove the joint from the pot and keep warm.
Strain the cooking liquor into a pan and bring to the boil. Blend the
cornflour with 1 tablespoon of water, then stir into the boiling stock.
Cook, stirring frequently, until thickened and smooth. Serve with the
joint, garnished with lemon wedges and sage leaves and freshly
cooked vegetables.

PORK GOULASH

ONE OF THE MAIN ADVANTAGES OF USING A SLOW COOKER IS THAT THE FOOD CAN BE LEFT TO SLOWLY SIMMER ALL DAY AND PART OF THE EVENING, IF NEED BE, WITHOUT ANY RISK OF BURNING.

SERVES	PREPARATION TIME	COOKING TIME	AUTO COOK
4	25 minutes	Cook on low 5 to 7 hours	7 to 9 hours

675 g/1½ lb lean pork, trimmed and cut into cubes

2 tbsp flour

Salt and freshly ground black pepper

2 tbsp sunflower oil

1 large onion, peeled and cut into wedges

2–4 garlic cloves, peeled and chopped

1 tbsp paprika

300 ml/½ pt vegetable or chicken stock

150 ml/¼ pt red wine

1 tbsp tomato purée

4 medium tomatoes, skinned and chopped

1 large orange pepper, deseeded and chopped

100 g/4 oz sliced button mushrooms

4 tbsp soured cream

2 tbsp snipped fresh chives

Cooked rice and a tossed green salad, to serve

1 Preheat the slow cooker on high. Toss the pork in the flour seasoned with salt and black pepper, reserving any excess flour. Heat the oil in a large pan and sauté the onion and garlic for 3 minutes. Remove from the pan with a slotted spoon and place in the cooking pot.

2 Add the flour-coated pork to the pan, sear on all sides, then sprinkle in any remaining flour and the paprika. Cook for 2 minutes. Take off the heat and gradually stir in the stock and the red wine. Add the tomato purée, chopped tomatoes and a little seasoning. Bring to the boil, stirring, then pour over the onions and garlic in the cooking pot and mix together. Cover, reduce the temperature to low and cook for 4 to 6 hours.

3 Cover the pepper and sliced mushrooms with boiling water, leave for 5 minutes, then drain and add to the cooking pot and continue to cook for 1 more hour. Stir well, then serve topped with the soured cream and sprinkled with the chives and accompanied by the freshly cooked rice and tossed green salad.

SWEET AND SOUR GAMMON

IT IS A GOOD IDEA TO SOAK SMOKED GAMMON JOINTS OVERNIGHT AS THIS HELPS TO REMOVE ANY EXCESS SALT. IT IS NOT NECESSARY TO SOAK UNSMOKED GAMMON, ALTHOUGH MANY BELIEVE THAT THIS IMPROVES THE FLAVOUR.

SERVES	PREPARATION TIME	COOKING TIME
6 to 8	10 minutes	Cook on high 3 to 5 hours

1.8-kg/4-lb gammon joint, soaked overnight if preferred

4 whole cloves

1 cinnamon stick, bruised

300 ml/½ pt orange juice

2 tbsp balsamic or red wine vinegar

1 tbsp maple syrup or clear honey

50 g/2 oz dried breadcrumbs, optional

50 g/2 oz demerara sugar

1 tbsp cornflour

Cooked rice or potatoes and vegetables, to serve

Chopped fresh herbs, to garnish

1 Preheat the cooker on high while preparing ingredients. Drain the gammon, if soaked overnight, then place in a large pan, cover with cold water and bring to the boil. Drain, rinse and place in the cooking pot with the cloves and cinnamon stick.

2 Blend the orange juice with the vinegar and maple syrup or honey and bring to the boil. Pour over the gammon, then cover with the lid and cook on high for 3 to 5 hours.

3 Once cooked, remove from the cooker and reserve the cooking liquor. Then cool the joint slightly and remove the rind. Either sprinkle with the breadcrumbs or score the fat and press the demerara sugar onto the fat. Place in a preheated hot oven, 400°F/200°C/Gas Mark 6 and cook for 15 to 20 minutes to crisp the topping.

4 Pour 300 ml/½ pint of the reserved cooking liquor into a small pan and bring to the boil. Blend the cornflour with 2 tablespoons of water or extra orange juice and pour into the boiling liquor. Cook, stirring, until the mixture thickens slightly, then pour over the gammon, sprinkle with chopped fresh herbs and serve with either freshly cooked rice or potatoes and vegetables.

LAMB RAGU

TRIM OFF AS MUCH FAT FROM THE LAMB AS POSSIBLE. ANY EXCESS FAT WILL
FLOAT TO THE TOP ONCE COOKED. YOU CAN THEN SKIM IT OFF BEFORE SERVING.

SERVES	PREPARATION TIME	COOKING TIME	AUTO COOK
4	30 minutes	Cook on low 6 to 8 hours	8 to 12 hours

675 g/1½ lb lamb fillet

2 tbsp flour

1 tbsp olive oil

1 large onion, peeled and chopped

2–4 garlic cloves, peeled and crushed

3 small leeks, trimmed and sliced

1 small butternut squash, peeled,
   deseeded and cut into small chunks

410-g/14½-oz can chopped tomatoes

1 tbsp tomato purée

150 ml/¼ pt stock

Salt and freshly ground black pepper

1 tsp dried marjoram or thyme

Fresh herb sprigs, to garnish

Freshly cooked pasta and tossed bitter
   leaf salad, to serve

1 Preheat the slow cooker on high. Trim the lamb and cut into small
   cubes, then toss in the flour, reserving any excess flour. Heat the oil
   in a frying pan and sauté the lamb for 5 minutes, stirring frequently,
   until browned. Remove with a slotted spoon and reserve.

2 Add the onion, garlic and two of the leeks to the frying pan and sauté
   for 5 minutes. Then sprinkle in any remaining flour and cook for 2
   minutes. Add the cubed squash and the canned chopped tomatoes.
   Blend the tomato purée with the stock, then add to the pan with
   seasoning to taste and the dried herbs. Bring to the boil, return the
   lamb to the pan, then spoon into the slow cooker cooking pot.

3 Cover with a lid, reduce the temperature and cook for 5½ hours.
   Cover the remaining leek with boiling water, leave for 5 minutes,
   then drain and add to the cooker. Continue to cook for 30 minutes
   to 2 hours before garnishing and serving with the freshly cooked
   pasta and salad.

LAMB HOT POT

DO NOT PEEK. THE MORE YOU RAISE THE LID, THE LONGER THE COOKING TIME!
REMOVING THE LID ADDS ABOUT 15 MINUTES TO THE OVERALL COOKING TIME.

SERVES	PREPARATION TIME	COOKING TIME	AUTO COOK
4	10 minutes	Cook on low 8 to 10 hours	10 to 12 hours

8–12 loin lamb chops, depending
   on size

4 large sweet potatoes, peeled and
   thinly sliced

2 medium onions, peeled and sliced

2 large carrots, peeled and sliced

4 celery stalks, trimmed and sliced

410-g/14½-oz can cannellini beans,
   rinsed and drained

2 large courgettes, trimmed and sliced

Salt and freshly ground black pepper

1 tsp dried mixed herbs

410-g/14½-oz can chopped tomatoes

75 g/3 oz pitted black olives

150 ml/¼ pt lamb or beef stock

1 tbsp unsalted butter, melted

1 tbsp chopped fresh parsley,
   to garnish

1 Preheat the slow cooker on high. Trim and discard any excess fat
   from each chop. Reserve a few sweet potatoes in a bowl of cold
   water. Place a layer of sliced sweet potatoes in the base of the
   cooking pot and top with a little sliced onion, carrot and celery. Place
   a layer of chops on top, with a few beans and courgette slices.
   Continue layering until all the vegetables and beans have been used,
   except for the reserved sweet potatoes, sprinkling each layer with
   salt, pepper and a little mixed herbs. Pour over the contents of the
   can of tomatoes. Add the olives, then pour over the stock. Drain the
   remaining sweet potatoes and arrange on top.

2 Cover, then reduce the temperature to low and cook for 8 to 10 hours
   or until tender. Brush the potatoes with the melted butter. Place under
   a preheated grill and cook for 4 to 6 minutes or until the potatoes are
   golden, sprinkle with the parsley and serve.

◄ Lamb Ragu

LAMB FILLET WITH PLUM SAUCE

THIS RECIPE IS SO SIMPLE TO PREPARE AND IT IS ABSOLUTELY DELICIOUS. IT WILL CERTAINLY BECOME AN ALL-TIME FAVOURITE.

SERVES	PREPARATION TIME	COOKING TIME	AUTO COOK
6	5 minutes	Cook on low 6 to 8 hours	8 to 10 hours

2 whole lamb fillets,
    about 675 g/1½ lb
2 tsp olive oil
2 tbsp Thai plum sauce
4 tbsp plum conserve
1 tbsp light soy sauce
1 tbsp balsamic vinegar
250 ml/8 fl oz orange juice
1 tbsp cornflour
Flat-leaf parsley and fresh sliced
    plums, to garnish
Cooked noodles and salad, to serve

1 Preheat the slow cooker on high. Trim the lamb fillets, heat the olive oil in a large frying pan and sear the fillets on all sides, remove from the pan and reserve.

2 Blend the Thai plum sauce with the plum conserve, the soy sauce and vinegar and heat gently. Brush over the top of each fillet, then place the fillets in the cooking pot. Pour over the orange juice, then spoon over any remaining plum sauce.

3 Cover with the lid, reduce the temperature and cook for 6 to 8 hours or until tender. Remove the fillets and keep warm. Strain the remaining sauce in the cooking pot into a small pan and boil until slightly reduced. Blend the cornflour with 2 tablespoons of water, stir into the sauce and cook, stirring, until thickened. Slice the fillets, arrange on individual serving plates, drizzle with a little sauce and garnish with the parsley and plums. Serve with freshly cooked noodles and salad.

LAMB WITH TAPENADE CRUST

THIS TAPENADE CAN BE USED AS A DIP AS WELL AS A STUFFING FOR THE LAMB.

SERVES	PREPARATION TIME	COOKING TIME
6 to 8	15 minutes	Cook on high 5 to 7 hours

150 g/6 oz pitted black olives
2 tbsp capers, drained
1 tbsp freshly chopped thyme
2 garlic cloves, peeled and crushed
1 tsp ready-made mustard
50 g/2 oz canned anchovy fillets
2 tbsp brandy
2–3 tbsp olive oil
50 g/2 oz soft breadcrumbs
1 small leg of lamb, boned
2 large onions, peeled and sliced
300 ml/½ pt tomato juice
Flat-leaf parsley, to garnish
Tomato and bitter leaf salad with
    chunks of warm crusty bread, to
    serve

1 Blend the olives, capers, thyme, garlic, mustard and anchovies with the anchovy oil in a food processor to form a thick purée. Gradually add the brandy with 1 tablespoon of the olive oil and the breadcrumbs and mix together.

2 Put the lamb on a chopping board and place half of the prepared tapenade in the centre. Fold the meat over to completely encase the stuffing and either tie or sew the lamb together.

3 Preheat the slow cooker on high. Heat the remaining olive oil in a large frying pan and brown the lamb on all sides. Add the onions to the oil remaining in the pan and sauté for 3 minutes. Drain thoroughly and place in the cooking pot. Spread the remaining tapenade over the top of the lamb and place on top of the onions.

4 Pour the tomato juice around the meat, cover and cook on high for 5 to 7 hours or until the lamb is tender. Serve with the braised onions, the cooking sauce, salad and crusty bread to soak up the juices.

▶ Lamb Fillet with Plum Sauce

BRAISED LAMB SHANKS

MAKE SURE THAT YOUR COOKER IS LARGE ENOUGH FOR THE SHANKS TO FIT IN COMFORTABLY. IF IT IS NOT, USE NECK FILLET RATHER THAN SHANKS.

SERVES	PREPARATION TIME	COOKING TIME
4	20 minutes	Cook on low 8 to 10 hours

2–4 small lamb shanks, depending
  on size
2 tbsp flour
1 tbsp sunflower oil
1 large onion, peeled and chopped
2–4 garlic cloves, peeled and chopped
2 celery stalks, trimmed and chopped
450 g/1 lb ripe tomatoes, chopped
75 g/3 oz Calamata olives
1 tsp dried oregano
Salt and freshly ground black pepper
250 ml/8 fl oz red wine
Fresh thyme sprigs, to garnish
Cooked potatoes and a tossed green
  salad, to serve

1 Preheat the slow cooker on high. Wipe the lamb shanks and coat them in flour.

2 Heat the oil in a large frying pan and brown the shanks on all sides. Remove and drain well before placing in the cooking pot.

3 Sprinkle over the chopped onion, garlic, celery, tomatoes and olives; then add the dried oregano and seasoning.

4 Blend the red wine with 4 tablespoons of water and pour over. Cover and reduce the temperature to low. Cook for 8 to 10 hours or until the meat is tender. Remove the meat and vegetables from the pot and place on a serving dish. Skim off any excess fat, garnish with thyme and serve with freshly cooked potatoes and a tossed green salad.

BEEF STROGANOFF

WHEN CUTTING UP THE STEAK FOR THIS RECIPE, TRY CUTTING IT INTO THIN STRIPS RATHER THAN CHUNKS.

SERVES	PREPARATION TIME	COOKING TIME	AUTO COOK
4	10 minutes	Cook on low 6 to 8 hours	8 to 10 hours

675 g/1½ lb good-quality braising
  steak, such as blade
2 tbsp flour
2 tbsp unsalted butter
1 large onion, peeled and sliced
2–3 garlic cloves, peeled and chopped
1 tbsp tomato purée
2 tsp ready-made mustard
450 ml/¾ pt beef stock
2 tbsp brandy
Salt and freshly ground black pepper
Freshly grated nutmeg, to taste
225 g/8 oz field mushrooms, wiped and
  sliced
150 ml/¼ pt soured cream
1 tbsp chopped fresh parsley,
  to garnish
Creamy mashed potatoes or buttered
  noodles and green salad, to serve

1 Preheat the slow cooker on high. Trim the steak and cut into strips and toss in the flour, reserving any remaining flour. Heat 1 tablespoon of the butter in a pan and brown the beef on all sides. Remove from the pan with a slotted spoon and place in the cooking pot.

2 Add about half of the remaining butter to the pan and gently sauté the onion and garlic for 3 minutes. Then sprinkle in any remaining flour and cook gently for a further 2 minutes.

3 Blend the tomato purée and mustard with the beef stock, pour into the pan and bring to the boil, stirring. Add the brandy with the seasoning and the nutmeg, then pour over the steak and cover with the lid.

4 Reduce the temperature to low and cook for 6 to 8 hours. One hour before the end of cooking time, heat the remaining butter and gently sauté the mushrooms, then add to the pan with the soured cream. Serve sprinkled with the parsley and with creamy mashed potatoes or freshly cooked buttered noodles and a green salad.

BRAISED BEEF

CHEAPER CUTS OF MEAT ARE FULL OF FLAVOUR AND EXTREMELY TASTY BUT DO REQUIRE LONG SLOW COOKING. THIS IS WHERE THE SLOW COOKER COMES INTO ITS OWN, AS YOU DO NOT HAVE TO USE THE BEST CUT OF BEEF WHEN MAKING CASSEROLES.

SERVES	PREPARATION TIME	COOKING TIME	AUTO COOK
4	30 minutes	Cook on low 7 to 9 hours	9 to 12 hours

675 g/1½ lb braising steak, trimmed and diced

2 tbsp flour

Salt and freshly ground black pepper

1 tbsp sunflower oil

8 baby onions, peeled

2 garlic cloves, peeled and chopped

1 tbsp paprika

300 ml/½ pt beef stock

1 tbsp tomato purée

4 large tomatoes, chopped

Freshly grated nutmeg, to taste

1 large red pepper, deseeded and chopped

100 g/4 oz button mushrooms

4 tbsp soured cream

Creamy mashed potatoes and crisp green salad, to serve

1 Preheat the slow cooker on high. Toss the beef in the flour seasoned with salt and pepper until coated, reserving any excess flour. Heat the oil in a large pan and brown the beef on all sides; do this in batches. Remove from the pan with a slotted spoon and reserve.

2 Cut the onions in half if large, then add to the pan with the garlic and sauté, stirring frequently, for 5 minutes. Return the beef to the pan, sprinkle in any remaining flour, plus the paprika, and cook for 3 minutes. Take the pan off the heat, then gradually stir in the stock and the tomato purée blended with 2 tablespoons of water. Return to the heat and cook, stirring, until the liquid comes to the boil.

3 Remove from the heat and add the chopped tomatoes. Add a little seasoning with the freshly grated nutmeg, place in the cooking pot, cover and cook on low for 5 hours.

4 Blanch the red pepper in boiling water for 2 minutes, then drain. Slice the mushrooms in half, if large, then add the pepper and mushrooms to the pot. Continue to cook for 2 to 4 hours.

5 Adjust the seasoning and serve with spoonfuls of soured cream and plenty of creamy mashed potatoes and a crisp green salad.

4

POULTRY

CHICKEN WITH COUSCOUS AND CRANBERRY STUFFING

IF A THICKER SAUCE IS PREFERRED, BLEND 2 TEASPOONS OF CORNFLOUR WITH 1 TABLESPOON OF WATER, STIR INTO A BOILING LIQUOR AND COOK, STIRRING UNTIL THICKENED.

SERVES	PREPARATION TIME	COOKING TIME
4	15 minutes	Cook on high 4 to 6 hours

4 large boneless chicken breasts

50 g/2 oz instant couscous

25 g/1 oz dried cranberries

2–3 spring onions, trimmed and finely chopped

25 g/1 oz chopped pecans

1 tbsp grated orange zest

½ tsp dried tarragon

Salt and freshly ground black pepper

1 large egg yolk, beaten

300 ml/½ pt orange juice

2 tbsp prepared cranberry sauce

2 tbsp light soy sauce

Freshly chopped herbs, to garnish

Freshly cooked vegetables and saffron-flavoured rice, to serve

1 Preheat the slow cooker on high. Skin and discard the chicken skin if necessary and make a deep slit along the longest side of each breast to form a deep pocket. Place between two sheets of baking paper and gently beat with a mallet or rolling pin to flatten slightly. Take care not to tear the chicken.

2 Just cover the couscous with boiling water and leave until all the water has been absorbed. Stir in the dried cranberries, the spring onions, pecans, orange zest, tarragon and seasoning. Stir in sufficient egg to bind the stuffing together and use to fill each chicken pocket. Either sew with fine twine or press the edges firmly together.

3 Place in the cooking pot. Blend the orange juice with the cranberry sauce and soy sauce and pour over the chicken breasts. Cover and cook on high for 4 to 6 hours or until tender.

4 Drain off the liquor into a small pan, bring to the boil and boil for 2 to 3 minutes or until thickened slightly. Garnish the chicken and serve with the sauce, vegetables and rice.

MEXICAN CHICKEN DRUMSTICKS

THE ADDITION OF CHOCOLATE TO A CHICKEN DISH MAY SOUND STRANGE,
BUT IT IT IS DELICIOUS. MAKE SURE, HOWEVER, YOU USE GOOD-QUALITY
DARK CHOCOLATE AS OTHER TYPES JUST WILL NOT DO.

SERVES	PREPARATION TIME	COOKING TIME
4	30 minutes	Cook on high 3 to 5 hours

4–8 chicken drumsticks, skinned

1 tbsp sunflower oil

1 tbsp unsalted butter

1 onion, peeled and chopped

2–4 garlic cloves, peeled and chopped

1 red serrano chilli, deseeded and
    chopped

1 tbsp flour

1 tbsp tomato purée

450 ml/¾ pt chicken stock

4 tomatoes, peeled and chopped

50 g/2 oz dark chocolate

Salt and freshly ground black pepper

2 tbsp sesame seeds

Lime wedges, to garnish

Cooked rice and a tossed green salad,
    to serve

1 Preheat the slow cooker on high. Lightly rinse or wipe the chicken
drumsticks and pat dry on kitchen paper. Heat the oil and butter in a
frying pan, brown the drumsticks on all sides, drain and place in the
cooking pot.

2 Add the onion, garlic and chilli to the pan and sauté for 5 minutes or
until softened. Sprinkle in the flour and cook for 2 minutes, then take
off the heat. Blend the tomato purée with 2 tablespoons of the stock
and gradually stir into the pan with the remaining stock and the
chopped tomatoes. Add the chocolate with seasoning and bring to
the boil. Cook, stirring, until the sauce has thickened slightly, then
pour over the drumsticks. Cook on high for 3 to 5 hours. Remove
from the cooker, adjust the seasoning of the sauce, then pour over
the chicken. Sprinkle with the sesame seeds, garnish with lime
wedges and serve with freshly cooked rice and a green salad.

CAJUN DIRTY RICE

CAJUN COOKING RELIES HEAVILY ON THE SEASONINGS USED, USUALLY PAPRIKA, WHICH CONSISTS OF SWEET PEPPERS, HOT CHILLI SAUCE, COMBINED WITH WHITE AND BLACK PEPPERS, GARLIC, DRIED THYME AND OREGANO.

SERVES	PREPARATION TIME	COOKING TIME
4 to 6	15 minutes	Cook on high 2 to 4 hours

6 rashers streaky bacon, chopped

350 g/12 oz chicken livers

225 g/8 oz freshly minced pork

1 onion, peeled and finely chopped

2–4 garlic cloves, peeled and crushed

2 celery sticks, trimmed and finely chopped

1 red pepper, deseeded and chopped

900 ml/1½ pt chicken stock

1–2 tsp Cajun seasoning

Salt and freshly ground black pepper

¼ tsp cayenne pepper, or to taste

1 tsp paprika

225 g/8 oz easy-cook long grain rice

6 spring onions, trimmed and chopped, to garnish

1 Preheat the cooker on high while preparing the ingredients. Place the bacon in a non-stick frying pan and heat gently until the fat begins to run. Meanwhile, discard any sinew or gristle from the chicken livers and finely chop. Add the livers and minced pork to the pan and cook, stirring frequently, until seared. Stir in the onion, garlic, celery and pepper and continue to cook for 3 minutes, stirring frequently.

2 Pour in the stock with the seasonings and rice and bring to the boil, then spoon into the cooking pot. Cover with the lid and cook on high for 2 to 4 hours. Adjust seasoning and serve sprinkled with the chopped spring onions.

CHICKEN HOT POT

IF PREFERRED SUBSTITUTE THE PARSNIPS WITH SWEET POTATOES.

SERVES	PREPARATION TIME	COOKING TIME
4	25 minutes	Cook on high 2 hours then low 3 to 6 hours

450 g/1 lb chicken thighs, skinned

2 tbsp unsalted butter

1 medium onion, peeled and thinly sliced

2–4 garlic cloves, peeled and crushed

1 tsp dried mixed herbs

450 g/1 lb potatoes, peeled and thinly sliced

2 large carrots, peeled and sliced

2 medium parsnips, peeled and sliced

3 celery sticks, trimmed and chopped

Salt and freshly ground black pepper

600 ml/1 pt chicken stock

Freshly chopped parsley, to garnish

1 Preheat the slow cooker on high. Discard any fat from the chicken thighs and dice. Heat 1 tablespoon of the butter in a frying pan, sear the chicken on all sides, remove and drain on kitchen paper. Add the sliced onion and garlic to the butter remaining in the pan and sauté for 3 minutes. Add the herbs and mix well, then remove from the heat.

2 Place a layer of the potatoes in the base of the cooking pot, top with a layer of carrot, parsnip and celery; season lightly between each layer. Place the chicken thighs on top and then the onion mixture. Continue the layering of the vegetables, finishing with a layer of potatoes. Bring the stock to the boil, then pour over the chicken and vegetables. Place the cooking pot in the cooker, cover and cook for 2 hours on high. Reduce the temperature to low and continue to cook for 3 to 6 hours.

3 Remove the lid, melt the remaining butter and use to brush over the potatoes. Place under a preheated grill and cook for 3 to 4 minutes or until golden. Serve garnished with parsley.

FLORIDA CHICKEN

THIS RECIPE IS TRULY EFFORTLESS. ONCE IN THE COOKER, THE FOOD SIMPLY COOKS ITSELF. ALL YOU NEED TO ADD IS SOME BREAD OR NEW POTATOES AND A SALAD – AND YOUR MEAL IS READY TO TAKE TO THE TABLE.

SERVES	PREPARATION TIME	COOKING TIME
4	15 minutes	Cook on high 3 to 5 hours

4 chicken quarters

1 tbsp oil

1 tbsp unsalted butter

300 ml/½ pt orange juice

1 tbsp grated orange and lemon rind

2 tbsp light soy sauce

1 tbsp orange blossom honey

½–1 tsp dried crushed chillies

2 tsp cornflour

Fresh herbs, to garnish

Warm crusty bread or freshly cooked new potatoes and roasted vegetables, to serve

1 Preheat the slow cooker on high. Wipe the chicken quarters, heat the oil and butter in a large frying pan and brown the chicken all over. Remove and drain well on kitchen paper, then arrange in the slow cooker cooking pot.

2 Blend the orange juice with the orange and lemon rind, soy sauce, honey and crushed chillies, then pour over the chicken. Cover with the lid and cook on high for 3 to 5 hours. Drain off the cooking liquor into a small pan and bring to the boil. Blend the cornflour with 1 tablespoon of water, stir into the boiling sauce and cook until thickened. Garnish the chicken with the herbs and serve with the sauce, bread or new potatoes and roasted vegetables.

POT ROAST CHICKEN WITH CUCUMBER SAUCE

THIS IS A VARIATION ON AN OLD RECIPE THAT WOULD HAVE USED BOILING FOWL. USING CHICKEN INSTEAD REPRODUCES THE FLAVOUR JUST AS WELL.

SERVES	PREPARATION TIME	COOKING TIME
4 to 6	20 minutes	Cook on high 4 to 5 hours

1.5-kg/3-lb whole chicken

1 lemon, preferably unwaxed or organic

Salt and freshly ground black pepper

1 tbsp sunflower oil

1 tbsp unsalted butter

1 shallot, peeled and finely chopped

1 small cucumber, peeled, deseeded and diced

150 ml/¼ pt medium dry white wine

150 ml/¼ pt chicken stock

1 tbsp cornflour

4–5 tbsp double cream

Fresh herbs and cucumber, to garnish

Cooked vegetables, to serve

1 Preheat the slow cooker on high. Lightly rinse or wipe the chicken and dry with kitchen paper. Cut the lemon into small wedges, then season the cavity of the chicken and place the lemon wedges inside. Heat the oil and butter in a frying pan, then brown the chicken on all sides. Remove and place in the cooking pot and scatter over the shallot and cucumber. Heat the wine and stock to almost boiling, then pour over the chicken. Cover and cook on high for 4 to 5 hours or until tender.

2 Remove the chicken from the pot and keep warm while preparing the sauce. Pour 250 ml/8 fl oz of the cooking liquor with the cucumber into a small pan and bring to the boil. Blend the cornflour with 1 tablespoon of water, then pour into the boiling liquor. Cook, stirring, until the mixture thickens. Stir in the cream and cook for 1 minute before adding seasoning to taste. Garnish the chicken and serve with the sauce and freshly cooked vegetables.

◀ Florida Chicken

GUINEA FOWL WITH ORANGE SAUCE

YOU CAN USE POUSSIN, PHEASANT OR EVEN CHICKEN PORTIONS FOR THIS
RECIPE. IF USING PHEASANT, ONE WILL FEED TWO PEOPLE AND WITH POUSSIN,
YOU WILL PROBABLY NEED ONE EACH.

SERVES	PREPARATION TIME	COOKING TIME
4	15 minutes	Cook on high 3 to 4 hours

1 tbsp unsalted butter

1.3-kg/3-lb oven-ready guinea fowl, jointed

Salt and freshly ground black pepper

6 rashers bacon, chopped

2 tsp sunflower oil

2 shallots, peeled and chopped

2 tbsp flour

150 ml/¼ pt orange juice

150 ml/¼ pt white wine

1 tbsp soy sauce

2–3 tbsp orange marmalade

225 g/8 oz peeled chestnuts

Fresh raspberries and herbs, to garnish

Crisps and cooked vegetables, to serve

1 Preheat the slow cooker on high. Wipe the cooking pot with a little of the butter. Wipe or lightly rinse the guinea fowl, pat dry and season. Melt the remaining butter in a frying pan and brown the guinea fowl on all sides. Remove, drain and place in the cooking pot. Add the bacon to the frying pan and cook for 2 minutes.

2 Add the oil to the pan and sauté the shallots for 2 minutes, take off the heat and sprinkle in the flour. Cook for 2 minutes, then gradually stir in the orange juice, white wine, soy sauce, marmalade, chestnuts and seasoning. Cook, stirring, until the sauce comes to the boil, then pour over the guinea fowl and cook for 3 to 4 hours. Skim off any excess fat. Serve the guinea fowl with the sauce scattered with the raspberries and herbs and accompanied by crips and freshly cooked vegetables.

TERIYAKI POUSSIN

WHEN COOKING POULTRY, WITH VERY FEW EXCEPTIONS, IT IS IMPORTANT THAT
THE SETTING ON YOUR SLOW COOKER IS ON HIGH. THIS ENSURES THAT THE
POULTRY IS COOKED THROUGH THOROUGHLY.

SERVES	PREPARATION TIME	COOKING TIME
4	5 minutes	Cook on high 3 to 5 hours

4 poussin, about 450 g/1 lb each

Salt and freshly ground black pepper

225 g/8 oz canned pineapple chunks, reserving juice

Few sprigs fresh coriander

150 ml/¼ pt teriyaki sauce

2 tbsp honey

Fresh coriander sprigs and spring onion tassels, to garnish

Cooked white and wild rice, to serve

1 Preheat the slow cooker on high. Lightly rinse or wipe the poussins and season the cavities. Drain the pineapple, reserving the juice and stuff the pineapple chunks into the poussin cavities together with a few sprigs of coriander. Place in the cooking pot.

2 Blend the canned pineapple juice with the teriyaki sauce and honey, bring to the boil and pour over the poussins. Cover with a lid and cook on high for 3 to 5 hours. Remove from the pot and serve garnished with coriander sprigs and spring onion tassels and with the freshly cooked rice. For a thicker sauce, bring the liquid to the boil and stir in 1 tablespoon of cornflour blended with 2 tablespoons of water; cook, stirring, until thickened.

CHICKEN GUMBO SUPPER

THIS RECIPE IS A COMPLETE MEAL IN ITSELF. YOU REALLY DO NOT NEED TO ADD
ANYTHING ELSE, JUST THE FAMILY OR FRIENDS TO SIT AND ENJOY.

SERVES	PREPARATION TIME	COOKING TIME
6	15 minutes	Cook on high 2 hours then low 4 to 6 hours

450 g/1 lb boned, skinned chicken thighs

4 thick garlic sausages such as Toulouse

1 tbsp olive oil

1 medium onion, peeled and chopped

2–4 garlic cloves, peeled and chopped

2 red serrano chillies, deseeded and chopped

2 celery stalks, trimmed and sliced

2 large carrots, peeled and diced

410-g/14$\frac{1}{2}$-oz can chopped tomatoes

250 ml/8 fl oz chicken stock

Salt and freshly ground black pepper

1 tsp dried thyme

1 red pepper, deseeded and chopped

225 g/8 oz okra, trimmed and thickly sliced

Hot pepper sauce, to taste

225 g/8 oz cooked long-grain rice

Flat leaf parsley sprigs, to garnish

Corn bread and tossed green salad, to serve

1 Preheat the slow cooker on high. Cut the chicken thighs and sausages into bite-sized pieces and place in the cooking pot. Add the remaining ingredients except the red pepper, okra, hot pepper sauce and rice. Cover and cook on high for 2 hours then reduce the temperature to low and continue to cook for 3 hours.

2 Meanwhile, cover the red pepper with boiling water, drain and add to the cooker with the okra, hot pepper sauce and the cooked rice. Continue to cook for 1 to 3 hours until tender. Garnish and serve with corn bread, tossed green salad and extra hot pepper sauce.

TURKEY TAGINE

THIS RECIPE TAKES ITS INSPIRATION FROM MOROCCO AND, TO CONTINUE WITH THE THEME, IT IS SERVED WITH COUSCOUS.

SERVES	PREPARATION TIME	COOKING TIME
4	25 minutes	Cook on high 3 to 5 hours

450 g/1 lb diced turkey meat

2 tbsp flour

Salt and freshly ground black pepper

2 tbsp sunflower oil

1 medium onion, peeled and cut into wedges

3–4 garlic cloves, peeled and sliced

1 tsp ground cumin

1 tsp ground coriander

1 cinnamon stick, lightly bashed

Large pinch of saffron

2 large carrots, peeled and sliced

300 ml/½ pt turkey or chicken stock

75 g/3 oz chopped dried apricots

3 tomatoes, chopped

410-g/14½-oz can chick peas, drained

1 tbsp chopped fresh coriander

Steamed couscous and bread or green salad, to serve

1 Preheat the slow cooker on high. Trim and discard any sinew or fat from the meat, then toss in the flour seasoned with salt and pepper. Heat 1 tablespoon of the oil in a pan and gently sauté the onion and garlic for 3 minutes. With a slotted spoon, transfer to the cooking pot.

2 Add the remaining oil to the pan and sear the turkey meat on all sides. Sprinkle in the ground spices with the cinnamon stick and saffron, add the carrots and cook, stirring frequently, for 3 minutes. Add the stock, stirring throughout. Bring to the boil, add the apricots and tomatoes, then pour over the onions in the cooking pot and mix lightly.

3 Cover the cooking pot with the lid and cook for 2 hours. Add the drained chick peas and continue to cook for another 1 to 3 hours. Remove the cinnamon stick, stir in the chopped coriander and serve with the freshly prepared couscous and bread or a green salad.

DUCK WITH CHERRIES

IF USING A FROZEN DUCK, ENSURE IT IS THOROUGHLY THAWED. IF YOU ARE IN A RUSH, SUBMERGE THE DUCK, STILL IN ITS WRAPPINGS, IN COLD WATER.

SERVES	PREPARATION TIME	COOKING TIME
4	15 minutes	Cook on high 4 to 5 hours

1.7- kg/4-lb oven-ready duck

1 small apple

1 small onion, peeled and cut into wedges

1 tbsp unsalted butter

410-g/14½-oz can sour cherries

1 tbsp white wine or balsamic vinegar

1 tbsp arrowroot

Salt and freshly ground black pepper

100 g/4 oz peeled, skinned and roughly chopped chestnuts

Fresh rocket and cherries, to garnish

Freshly cooked vegetables, to serve

1 Preheat the slow cooker on high. Discard any excess fat from inside the duck cavity and prick the skin with a fork. Rinse and pat dry with kitchen paper. Core the apple, then cut into wedges and place along with the onion wedges in the duck cavity. Melt the butter in a frying pan and brown the duck on all sides, then place in the cooking pot and cover. Cook on high for 3 hours. Drain off and discard the fat.

2 Drain the can of cherries into a measuring cup. Add water to the juice to make up to 300 ml/½ pint of liquid. Reserve the cherries. Pour the liquid into a small pan, stir in the vinegar and bring to the boil. Blend the arrowroot with 1 tablespoon of water, then stir into the boiling liquor. Cook, stirring, until the sauce thickens slightly. Add seasoning and the reserved cherries and chestnuts, then pour over the duck and continue to cook for 1 to 2 hours. Serve, garnished with rocket, cherries, if available, and freshly cooked vegetables.

CHICKEN RISOTTO

NORMALLY WHEN MAKING A RISOTTO YOU HAVE TO MAKE SURE THAT IT DOES NOT DRY OUT. WITH THE SLOW COOKER THIS IS NOT NECESSARY.

SERVES	PREPARATION TIME	COOKING TIME
4 to 6	15 minutes plus 20 minutes soaking time	Cook on high 3 to 5 hours

1 tbsp dried mushrooms

1 tbsp unsalted butter

3 shallots, cut into thin wedges

2–4 garlic cloves, peeled and crushed

¼–½ tsp saffron strands

1 tbsp grated lemon rind

350 g/12 oz fresh skinless, boneless chicken, diced

1¼ cups 225 g/8 oz easy-cook risotto rice

1¼ cups (300 ml) white wine

2½ cups 600 ml/1 pt chicken stock

75 g/3 oz sliced button mushrooms

3 tomatoes, deseeded and chopped

75 g/3 oz peas, thawed if frozen

Salt and freshly ground black pepper

2 tbsp chopped fresh chervil or parsley

Lemon wedges, to garnish

Freshly grated Parmesan, to serve

1 Preheat the cooker on high. Soak the dried mushrooms in almost boiling water for 20 minutes, then drain, reserving the soaking liquor. Heat the butter in a large frying pan; when melted, sauté the shallots and garlic for 2 minutes before sprinkling in the saffron strands, lemon rind and chicken. Cook, stirring, until the chicken is seared, then sprinkle in the rice and cook for 2 more minutes. Stir frequently. Pour in the wine and 450 ml/¾ pint of the stock, then strain the mushroom soaking liquor into the pan together with the soaked mushrooms, button mushrooms and tomatoes. Bring to the boil and spoon into the cooking pot. Cover with the lid and cook on high for 2 hours.

2 Add the peas and remaining stock if necessary and continue to cook for 1 to 3 hours. Adjust the seasoning to taste, stir in the chopped herbs and serve garnished with the lemon wedges and the Parmesan.

CHINESE STYLE DUCK

THIS IS THE NEAREST THAT YOU CAN GET TO A STIR-FRY IN YOUR SLOW COOKER. REDUCING THE TEMPERATURE TO LOW AFTER 1 HOUR KEEPS THE VEGETABLES REASONABLY CRISP.

SERVES	PREPARATION TIME	COOKING TIME
4	15 minutes	Cook on high 1 hour then low 3 to 4 hours

1 tbsp dried Chinese mushrooms

450 g/1 lb duck breast with fat removed

1 large carrot, peeled

2 celery stalks, trimmed

225 g/8 oz canned pineapple chunks

100 g/4 oz lychees, peeled and stoned if fresh

1 tbsp sunflower oil

1 red onion, peeled and cut into wedges

100 g/4 oz water chestnuts

1 tbsp hoisin sauce

2 tbsp light soy sauce

2 tbsp cornflour

4 spring onions, trimmed and shredded, to garnish

Fried rice, to serve

1 Preheat the slow cooker on high while preparing ingredients. Soak the mushrooms in almost boiling water for 20 minutes. Drain, reserving the liquor and mushrooms. Slice the mushrooms if large. Cut the duck breasts into thin strips, reserve, then cut the carrot and celery into matchsticks. Drain the pineapple, reserving the juice and flesh and cut the lychees in half.

2 Heat the oil in a frying pan and sauté the duck breasts until sealed. With a slotted spoon, transfer to the slow cooker cooking pot. Add the onion, carrots and celery to the pan and cook for 2 minutes, stirring frequently. Add the drained mushrooms and water chestnuts.

3 Blend the hoisin and soy sauce together and add to the pan. Blend the cornflour with the pineapple juice, stir in the reserved mushroom liquor, pour into the pan and bring to the boil. Cook, stirring, until thickened, then pour over the duck, cover and cook for 1 hour. Reduce the temperature, add the pineapple and lychees and continue to cook for 3 to 4 hours. Serve sprinkled with spring onions and with the freshly cooked fried rice.

CHICKEN WITH 40 GARLIC CLOVES

THE FRAGRANT AROMA THAT COMES FROM THE KITCHEN WHILE THIS DISH IS COOKING IS WONDERFUL. SERVE WITH PLENTY OF FRESH TOAST OR CRACKERS.

SERVES	PREPARATION TIME	COOKING TIME
4 to 6	10 minutes	Cook on high 3 to 5 hours

50 g/2 oz unsalted butter

1.5-kg/3-lb oven-ready chicken

Salt and freshly ground black pepper

40 whole unpeeled garlic cloves

Fresh herbs, to garnish

Fresh toast, hot rice and ratatouille, to serve

1 Preheat the slow cooker on high and wipe the cooking pot with a little of the butter. Wipe or lightly rinse the chicken and pat dry with kitchen paper then season and stuff the cavity with about half the garlic cloves.

2 Melt half of the butter in a frying pan and brown the chicken all over. Remove and place in the cooking pot, then scatter over the remaining unpeeled garlic cloves. Melt the remaining butter and pour over the chicken, cover and cook on high for 3 to 5 hours. Serve the chicken with the garlic, garnished with herbs and accompanied by the toast, rice and ratatouille.

TURKEY WITH WINE AND PEPPERS

ALTHOUGH THIS IS A CASSEROLE STYLE DISH, IT WOULD BE IDEAL TO SERVE FOR EITHER A FORMAL OR FAMILY OCCASION. SIMPLY VARY THE ACCOMPANIMENTS.

SERVES	PREPARATION TIME	COOKING TIME
4	15 minutes	Cook on high 3 to 5 hours

550 g/1½ lb turkey breast

2 tbsp flour

Salt and freshly ground black pepper

2 tbsp sunflower oil

1 large white onion, peeled and cut into wedges

3–4 garlic cloves, peeled and crushed

6 bacon rashers, chopped

1 red pepper, deseeded and sliced

1 yellow pepper, deseeded and sliced

3 tbsp brandy

250 ml/8 fl oz red wine

120 ml/4 fl oz turkey or chicken stock

Fresh rocket leaves, to garnish

Creamed potatoes, green vegetables and carrots, or salad and crusty bread, to serve

1 Preheat the slow cooker on high while preparing the ingredients. Trim the turkey of any sinew or fat, then cut into bite-sized pieces. Season the flour with salt and pepper, then toss over the turkey, reserving any remaining flour.

2 Heat 1 tablespoon of the oil in a large pan and sauté the turkey until seared all over, remove from the pan and reserve. Add the remaining oil to the pan and sauté the onion, garlic and bacon for 3 minutes. Add the peppers and any remaining flour to the pan and continue to cook, stirring, for 1 minute. Return the turkey to the pan, add the brandy and heat for 1 minute. Take the pan off the heat and set alight. When all the flames have subsided, gradually stir in the wine and stock. Return to the heat and cook, stirring, until the mixture comes to the boil. Carefully pour into the cooking pot.

3 Cover and cook on high for 3 to 5 hours. Adjust the seasoning. Serve garnished with rocket leaves and accompanied by the potatoes and freshly cooked vegetables or a salad and crusty bread to mop up all the juices.

DUCK JAMBALAYA

JAMBALAYA WAS CREATED IN THE 18TH CENTURY AND IS A CAJUN/CREOLE DISH. IT NORMALLY CONTAINS PORK, USUALLY IN THE FORM OF CHORIZO, A HOT SPICY SAUSAGE. HOWEVER, THERE ARE NO RULES, SO ADD WHAT TAKES YOUR FANCY.

SERVES	PREPARATION TIME	COOKING TIME
4 to 6	20 minutes	Cook on high 2 to 4 hours

3 boneless duck breasts

4 slices smoked fatty bacon, chopped

1 white onion, peeled and chopped

2–4 garlic cloves, peeled and crushed

2 celery sticks, trimmed and chopped

1 green pepper, deseeded and chopped

410-g/14½-oz can chopped tomatoes

Hot pepper sauce, to taste

Pinch cayenne pepper

Freshly ground black pepper

175 g/6 oz easy-cook brown rice

50 g/2 oz wild rice

225 g/8 oz chorizo, or other spicy sausage, cut into chunks

1 tsp dried thyme

2–3 tsp Worcestershire sauce

900 ml/1½ pints chicken stock

Diagonally sliced spring onions, to garnish

1 Preheat the cooker on high while preparing the ingredients. Remove the fat from the duck breasts and cut into slices. Place the bacon into a non-stick frying pan and cook gently until the fat begins to run out. Add the duck pieces and brown all over, then remove and reserve.

2 Add the onion, garlic, celery and green pepper to the pan and cook gently for 3 minutes, stirring frequently. Return the duck to the pan, then add all the other ingredients except the spring onions. Bring to the boil and pour into the cooking pot. Cover with the lid and cook on high for 2 to 4 hours, adjust seasoning and serve sprinkled with sliced spring onions.

TURKEY MOLE

YOU CAN SERVE THIS EITHER AS A FILLING FOR TACOS OR BURRITOS OR
ACCOMPANIED BY CORN BREAD, RICE, GUACAMOLE, OR SOURED CREAM.

SERVES	PREPARATION TIME	COOKING TIME
4 to 6	30 minutes	Cook on high 3 to 5 hours

6 dried pasilla chillies

20 whole blanched almonds

2 tbsp pine kernels

Small piece cinnamon stick

3 whole cloves

1 onion, peeled and sliced

2 garlic cloves, peeled and crushed

2½ tbsp toasted sesame seeds

1 tsp ground coriander

Freshly ground black pepper

2 tbsp sunflower oil

300 ml/½ pt chicken stock

410-g/14½-oz can chopped tomatoes

50 g/2 oz plain dark chocolate

450 g/1 lb boneless, skinless turkey
   thighs, diced

Sesame seeds, spring onions, to garnish

Tomato and red onion salad, to serve

1 Preheat the cooker on high, 20 minutes before cooking. Rehydrate the dried chillies in almost boiling water and leave for at least 20 minutes, longer if time permits. Drain the chillies and place in a food processor with the almonds, pine kernels, cinnamon, cloves, onion, garlic, sesame seeds, coriander and black pepper and blend to form a paste. Heat 1 tablespoon of the oil in a frying pan and fry the paste for 5 minutes. Stir frequently. Add the stock and tomatoes, then simmer for 10 minutes. Add the chocolate and cook until the chocolate has melted. Remove from the heat and reserve.

2 Meanwhile, heat the remaining oil in a large pan and sear the turkey on all sides. Add to the reserved sauce then spoon into the cooking pot. Cook for 3 to 5 hours. Serve sprinkled with extra sesame seeds, sliced spring onions and a tomato and red onion salad.

CHICKEN WITH PASTA

TRY ADDING TOASTED PINE KERNELS, LEMON RIND AND MINT – OR CHOPPED DRIED
APRICOTS, FRESH CORIANDER AND ORANGE RIND WITH A FEW CHOPPED PECANS.

SERVES	PREPARATION TIME	COOKING TIME
4	10 minutes	Cook on high 1 hour then low 4 to 5 hours

450 g/1 lb minced chicken

6 spring onions, finely chopped

2 garlic cloves, peeled and crushed

4 sundried tomatoes, drained if in oil
   and finely chopped

1tbsp tomato purée

Salt and freshly ground black pepper

1 tsp dried oregano

50 g/2 oz fresh brown breadcrumbs

1 large egg, beaten

410-g/14½-oz can chopped tomatoes

1 small onion, peeled and grated

2 tsp Worcestershire sauce

Fresh oregano sprigs, to garnish

Cooked pasta, grated Parmesan, warm
   Italian style bread and tossed bitter
   leaf salad, to serve

1 Preheat the slow cooker on high. Mix together the minced chicken, spring onions, garlic, sundried tomatoes, tomato purée, seasoning and the dried oregano. Add the breadcrumbs, then bind together with the beaten egg. Shape into small meatballs and place in the slow cooker cooking pot.

2 Blend the chopped tomatoes and their juice with the grated onion, Worcestershire sauce and seasoning, then pour over the meatballs. Cover and cook on high for 1 hour, then reduce the heat to low and cook for 4 to 5 hours. Skim off any excess oil. Serve on the freshly cooked pasta with grated Parmesan cheese and oregano sprigs, accompanied by warm bread and tossed salad.

ROSÉ CHICKEN

ROSÉ WINE IS USED IN THIS RECIPE, HENCE THE NAME—BUT IT WILL WORK PERFECTLY WITH EITHER RED OR WHITE WINE. WHEN CHOOSING WINE FOR COOKING, DO NOT BE TEMPTED TO USE WINE YOU WOULD NOT DRINK.

SERVES	PREPARATION TIME	COOKING TIME
4	20 minutes	Cook on high 3 to 5 hours

4 chicken portions

2 tbsp flour

2 tbsp unsalted butter

8–12 small onions, peeled

2–4 garlic cloves, peeled and cut into slivers

175-g/6-oz piece gammon, diced

2 tbsp brandy

250 ml/8 fl oz rosé wine

120 ml/4 fl oz chicken stock

2 bay leaves

1 fresh bouquet garni

Salt and freshly ground black pepper

100 g/4 oz button mushrooms

1 tbsp chopped fresh parsley

Creamed potatoes flavoured with spring onions and green salad, to serve

1 Preheat the slow cooker on high. Wipe or rinse the chicken portions and pat dry with kitchen paper. Coat in the flour and reserve both any excess flour and the chicken. Heat the butter in a frying pan and sauté the onions, garlic and gammon for 3 minutes. Remove with a slotted spoon and place in the cooking pot.

2 Add the chicken to the butter remaining in the frying pan, sear the chicken on all sides, add the brandy, heat for 1 minute, then set alight. Once the flames have subsided, remove the chicken from the pan and place in the cooking pot.

3 Sprinkle in the reserved flour, cook for 2 minutes, then draw off the heat and gradually stir in the wine, then the stock. Bring to the boil and pour over the chicken. Add the bay leaves, bouquet garni and seasoning, then cover and cook on high for 2 hours.

4 Add the mushrooms and cook for another 1 to 3 hours. Remove the bouquet garni and bay leaves, skim off any excess fat, adjust the seasoning, sprinkle with the chopped parsley and serve with creamed potatoes and salad.

CHAPTER FIVE

VEGETABLES

PEPPER AND RED KIDNEY BEAN RICE

EASY-COOK BROWN RICE STANDS UP BEST OF ALL TO THE LONG SLOW COOKING. IF COOKING FOR VEGETARIANS, SUBSTITUTE 1 TSP CONCENTRATED VEGETABLE BOUILLON FOR THE THAI FISH SAUCE.

SERVES	PREPARATION TIME	COOKING TIME	AUTO COOK
4 to 6	10 minutes plus 20 minutes soaking	Cook on high 4 to 5 hours	6 to 8 hours

1 tbsp dried shiitake mushrooms

1 tbsp groundnut oil

4 shallots, peeled and cut into wedges

2–4 garlic cloves, peeled and chopped

1–2 bird's eye chillies, deseeded, chopped

175 g (6 oz) easy-cook brown rice, rinsed

1 lemon grass stalk, outer leaves discarded, chopped

2 kaffir lime leaves, crumbled if dried

2 small red peppers, deseeded and chopped

600 ml/1 pt vegetable stock

1 tbsp light soy sauce

2 tsp Thai fish sauce

1 tsp honey

200 g/7 oz canned red kidney beans, drained and rinsed

225 g/8 oz sliced button mushrooms

1 tbsp chopped fresh coriander

Green salad, to serve

1 Preheat the slow cooker on high while preparing the ingredients. Soak the dried mushrooms in almost boiling water for 20 minutes, drain, reserving the liquor. Heat the oil in a pan and sauté the shallots, garlic and chillies for 3 minutes. Add the rice, lemon grass, kaffir lime leaves, red pepper, stock, soy and fish sauces, reserved soaked mushrooms and their liquor and honey. Bring to the boil. Pour into the cooking pot and cook for 3 hours.

2 Add the kidney beans and button mushrooms and continue to cook for 1 to 2 hours. Sprinkle with coriander and serve with a green salad.

VEGETABLE GOULASH

USE ANY SQUASH FOR THIS RECIPE BUT TAKE CARE WITH SOME OF THE
VARIETIES AS THE OUTER SKIN CAN BE TOUGH AND DIFFICULT TO CUT THROUGH.

SERVES	PREPARATION TIME	COOKING TIME	AUTO COOK
4	30 minutes	Cook on low 6 to 8 hours	8 to 12 hours

1 tbsp olive oil

1 large onion, peeled and cut
    into wedges

2–4 garlic cloves, peeled and crushed

3 celery sticks, trimmed and sliced

3 medium carrots, peeled and sliced

1 small butternut squash, or 2 acorn
    squash, peeled and diced

300 g/10 oz new potatoes, scrubbed

225 g/8 oz cauliflower florets

1 tbsp hot paprika

1 tbsp flour

410-g/14½-oz can cannellini beans,
    drained

600 ml/1 pt tomato juice

150 ml/¼ pt vegetable stock

1 tsp dried thyme

½–1 tsp caraway seeds

Salt and freshly ground black pepper

Thyme sprigs, to garnish

Roasted vine tomatoes, crusty bread
    and soured cream, to serve

1 Preheat the slow cooker on high. Heat the oil in a frying pan and
   sauté the onion, garlic and celery for 3 minutes. Add the remaining
   vegetables, sprinkle in the paprika and flour and continue to sauté for
   5 more minutes. Place in the cooking pot and stir in the beans.

2 Blend the tomato juice with the stock and bring to the boil. Stir in the
   dried thyme, caraway seeds and seasoning, then pour over the
   vegetables in the pot. Cover, reduce the temperature to low and cook
   for 6 to 8 hours. Garnish with thyme sprigs and serve with roasted
   vine tomatoes, crusty bread and soured cream.

STUFFED PEPPERS

THESE STUFFED PEPPERS PROVED A GREAT SUCCESS. THE STUFFING IS SO GOOD AND VERSATILE THAT IT CAN BE USED TO STUFF AUBERGINE AND COURGETTE.

SERVES	PREPARATION TIME	COOKING TIME
4	15 minutes	Cook on high 2 to 4 hours

4 assorted coloured peppers

75 g/3 oz instant couscous

6 spring onions, trimmed and chopped

50 g/2 oz raisins

1 tbsp grated lemon rind

$\frac{1}{4}$–1 tsp dried crushed chillies, according to taste

2 tomatoes, deseeded and chopped

50 g/2 oz strong-flavoured cheese, such as Cheddar cheese, grated

2 tbsp toasted pine kernels

1 tbsp chopped fresh flat-leaf parsley

Salt and freshly ground black pepper

1 large egg, beaten

150 ml/$\frac{1}{4}$ pt vegetable stock

Flat-leaf parsley, to garnish, optional

Preheat the slow cooker on high. Cut the peppers either in half lengthways or cut off the tops to form a lid. Remove and discard the seeds and membrane, then cover with boiling water and leave for 5 minutes, drain and reserve. Meanwhile place the couscous in a bowl, cover with boiling water and leave until all the water has been absorbed. Add the chopped spring onions, raisins, lemon rind, chillies, tomatoes, cheese, pine kernels, parsley and seasoning to taste. Mix well, then bind together with the beaten egg. Use to stuff the peppers, then place in the cooking pot. Heat the stock and pour around the peppers, cover with the lid and cook on high for 2 to 4 hours. Serve, if like, garnished with flat-leaf parsley.

COURGETTES WITH APPLE AND HAZELNUT STUFFING

THIS STUFFING COULD BE USED TO STUFF ANY VEGETABLES, BUT IT IS GREAT WITH SQUASH. FOR A CHANGE, SERVE IT WITH A FRESH TANGY TOMATO SAUCE, PAGE 30.

SERVES	PREPARATION TIME	COOKING TIME
4	15 minutes	Cook on low 4 to 6 hours

4 medium-sized courgettes

1 tbsp butter

2 shallots, peeled and chopped

2–3 garlic cloves, peeled and crushed

1 medium apple, peeled and grated

50 g/2 oz chopped hazelnuts

50 g/2 oz soft breadcrumbs

75 g/3 oz strong-flavoured grated cheese such as Swiss or Cheddar

Salt and freshly ground black pepper

1 tsp dried sage

2 medium eggs, beaten

150 ml/$\frac{1}{4}$ pt apple juice

Apple sauce, to serve

Apple slices and fresh sage, to garnish

1 Preheat the cooker on high. Peel the courgettes, cut in half lengthways and discard the seeds. Heat the butter in a small pan and sauté the shallots and garlic for 2 minutes, remove from the heat and stir in the apple, hazelnuts, breadcrumbs, two-thirds of the cheese, seasoning and the sage. Mix to a stiff consistency with the egg. Use to stuff the courgettes.

2 Place the stuffed vegetables in the cooking pot, sprinkle with the remaining cheese and pour around the apple juice. Cook on low for 4 to 6 hours. Serve with the apple sauce, garnished with the apple slices and fresh sage. If liked, place the cooked courgettes under a preheated grill, sprinkle the tops with a little extra cheese and grill to brown the top.

WARM BEAN AND PUMPKIN SALAD

THE SPINACH COOKS SO QUICKLY THAT IT IS ADDED RIGHT AT THE VERY END OF THE COOKING TIME. YOU COULD USE FROZEN SPINACH, BUT FRESH IS DEFINITELY BETTER. FOR A CHANGE, USE SWISS CHARD IN PLACE OF THE SPINACH.

SERVES	PREPARATION TIME	COOKING TIME	AUTO COOK
6	30 minutes plus overnight soaking	Cook on low 8 to 10 hours	10 to 12 hours

100 g/4 oz dried haricot beans, soaked overnight

100 g/4 oz dried red kidney beans, soaked overnight

100 g/4 oz dried black-eye beans, soaked overnight

2 tbsp olive oil

1 large onion, peeled and cut into wedges

Small piece fresh root ginger, peeled and grated

2–4 garlic cloves, peeled and chopped

$\frac{1}{4}$–1 tsp dried crushed chillies

1 tsp cumin seeds

1 tsp ground coriander

$\frac{1}{2}$ tsp turmeric

450 g/1 lb pumpkin, peeled, deseeded and diced

300 ml/$\frac{1}{2}$ pint vegetable stock

100 g/4 oz cherry tomatoes, quartered

175 g/6 oz spinach, thoroughly washed and shredded

175 g/6 oz feta cheese, diced

Fresh coriander sprigs

Salt and freshly ground black pepper

Soured cream or low-fat natural yoghurt and warm pitta bread strips, to serve

1 Cover the beans with cold water and leave to soak overnight. Next day, drain, place in a pan and cover with water. Bring to the boil and boil for 10 minutes. Drain and reserve.

2 Preheat the slow cooker on high. Heat the oil in a frying pan and sauté the onion with the ginger, garlic, chillies to taste and all the spices for 3 minutes. Add the pumpkin and continue to sauté for 3 more minutes, then spoon into the cooking pot and stir in the drained beans. Heat the stock to boiling and pour over the vegetables and beans. Cover, reduce temperature to low, then cook for 8 to 10 hours.

3 Just before serving, stir in the tomatoes and spinach, stir well and continue to cook for 15 to 20 minutes or until the spinach has begun to wilt. Sprinkle with the diced feta cheese and the freshlly chopped coriander and serve with soured cream or yoghurt and strips of warm pitta bread.

MOROCCAN HOT POT

FRYING THE SPICES BEFORE COOKING IN THE COOKING POT INTENSIFIES THEIR FLAVOUR. IT IS IMPORTANT TO USE YOUR SPICES QUICKLY AS THEY CAN LOSE THEIR AROMA – BUY IN SMALL QUANTITIES AND STORE IN A COOL, DARK PLACE.

SERVES	PREPARATION TIME	COOKING TIME	AUTO COOK
6	15 minutes	Cook on low 4 to 6 hours	6 to 8 hours

1 tbsp olive oil

1 onion, peeled and cut into wedges

2–4 garlic cloves, peeled and chopped

1 red jalapeño chilli, deseeded and chopped

1 tsp cumin seeds

1 tsp ground coriander

$\frac{1}{4}$–$\frac{1}{2}$ tsp saffron or turmeric

2 medium carrots

350 g/12 oz baby aubergines, trimmed and halved or quartered if large

300 g/10 oz diced pattypan squash or similar

1 cinnamon stick, bruised

410-g/14$\frac{1}{2}$-oz can chopped tomatoes

150 ml/$\frac{1}{4}$ pint vegetable stock

50 g (2 oz) pitted prunes, chopped

Salt and freshly ground black pepper

410-g/14$\frac{1}{2}$-oz can chick peas, drained

4 baby courgettes, trimmed, halved, and blanched

2 tbsp chopped fresh coriander, to garnish

Freshly prepared couscous, to serve

1 Preheat the slow cooker while preparing the ingredients. Heat the oil in a frying pan and sauté the onion, garlic, chilli and spices for 3 minutes, stirring frequently. Add all the other vegetables, including the squash, and bruised cinnamon stick and place in the cooking pot.

2 Heat the chopped tomatoes with the stock, add the prunes, seasoning and chick peas, then pour over the vegetables in the pot and cover. Reduce the heat to low and cook for 3$\frac{1}{2}$ hours. Add the blanched, halved courgettes and cook for a further 30 minutes to 2 hours. Sprinkle with the chopped coriander and serve with the freshly prepared couscous.

SPICY VEGETABLES WITH COCONUT

VARY THE VEGETABLES ACCORDING TO PERSONAL TASTE AND AVAILABILITY. THERE IS A GROWING DEMAND FOR ORGANIC VEGETABLES AS THEY TASTE BETTER AND HAVE NOT BEEN SPRAYED OR TREATED WITH PESTICIDES.

SERVES	PREPARATION TIME	COOKING TIME	AUTO COOK
4 to 6	20 minutes	Cook on high 3 to 5 hours or low 5 to 8 hours	8 to 10 hours

2 tbsp sunflower oil

1 white onion, peeled and cut into wedges

2–4 garlic cloves, peeled and chopped

1–3 red serrano chillies, deseeded and chopped

Small piece root ginger, peeled and grated

1 tsp ground coriander

1 tsp turmeric

1 sweet potato, peeled and diced

1 small head cauliflower, divided into florets

2 carrots, peeled and sliced

1 red pepper, deseeded and chopped

4 tomatoes, peeled if preferred, deseeded and chopped

2 tbsp ground blanched almonds

150 ml/¼ pt vegetable stock

250 ml/8 fl oz coconut milk

Salt and freshly ground black pepper

2 tbsp chopped fresh coriander, to garnish

Cooked rice, to serve

1 Preheat the cooker on high while preparing the ingredients. Heat the oil in a frying pan and sauté the onion, garlic, chillies and root ginger for 2 minutes. Add the spices and continue to sauté for another 3 minutes. Add all the prepared vegetables, then blend the ground almonds with the stock and coconut milk and bring almost to boiling point, stirring throughout.

2 Spoon or pour into the cooking pot and add a little seasoning. Stir, cover and cook on high for 3 to 5 hours, or on low for 5 to 8 hours. Adjust seasoning, sprinkle with the chopped coriander and serve with the freshly cooked rice.

RATATOUILLE WITH KIDNEY BEANS

THIS RECIPE USES CANNED RED KIDNEY BEANS. YOU CAN USE DRIED, BUT
REMEMBER TO BOIL FOR 10 MINUTES AND GO EASY ON THE SEASONING, AS
TOO MUCH SALT DURING COOKING CAN TOUGHEN BEANS.

SERVES	PREPARATION TIME	COOKING TIME	AUTO COOK
4	15 minutes	Cook on high 4 to 5 hours	5 to 8 hours

1 tbsp olive oil

1 large onion, peeled and chopped

2–4 garlic cloves, peeled and chopped

1 large aubergine, trimmed and diced

450 g/1 lb chopped ripe plum tomatoes

1 red pepper, deseeded and chopped

1 yellow pepper, deseeded and
    chopped

410-g/14½-oz can red kidney beans,
    drained and rinsed

150 ml/¼ pt red wine or
    vegetable stock

Salt and freshly ground black pepper

175 g/6 oz sliced button mushrooms

2 courgettes, trimmed and sliced

2 tbsp chopped fresh basil

Fresh basil sprigs, to garnish

Freshly shaved Parmesan cheese and
    warm crusty bread, to serve

1 Preheat the slow cooker on high. Heat the oil in a frying pan and
   sauté the onion, garlic and aubergine for 5 minutes. Add all the
   remaining ingredients except for the mushrooms, courgette and
   1 tablespoon of the chopped basil and stir well. Spoon into the
   cooking pot and cover with the lid.

2 Cook on high for 3 hours, then add the mushrooms and courgettes
   and continue to cook for 1 to 3 more hours. Serve, garnished with the
   fresh basil sprigs and sprinkled with the remaining chopped basil,
   freshly shaved Parmesan cheese and crusty bread.

BARBECUED BEANS

YOU CAN REPLACE THE BLACK TREACLE WITH MAPLE SYRUP – THE BLACK
TREACLE GIVES A HEARTY FLAVOUR, WHILE THE USE OF MAPLE SYRUP GIVES
THE BEANS A MORE DELICATE FLAVOUR.

SERVES	PREPARATION TIME	COOKING TIME	AUTO COOK
4 to 6	15 minutes plus overnight soaking	Cook on low 8 to 10 hours	10 to 14 hours

225 g/8 oz dried haricot beans, soaked
   overnight

1 large onion, peeled and chopped

2–4 garlic cloves, peeled and crushed

6 tbsp tomato ketchup

1 tbsp black treacle

1 tbsp dark brown sugar

1 tsp ready-made wholegrain or
   English mustard

250 ml/8 fl oz vegetable stock

Coriander sprigs, to garnish

Warm bread, coleslaw and tomato
   salad, to serve

Cover the beans with cold water, cover and leave overnight. Next day,
preheat the cooker on high. Drain the beans, place in a pan, cover
with water and bring to the boil. Boil gently for 10 minutes, then
drain and place in the cooking pot. Add the chopped onion with the
garlic and stir well. Blend the tomato ketchup with the black treacle,
sugar, mustard and stock. Pour over the beans and stir well. Cover,
reduce the temperature to low and cook for 8 to 10 hours. Serve,
garnished with coriander sprigs and wedges of warm bread, coleslaw
and tomato salad.

STUFFED ACORN SQUASH

THESE LOVELY SQUASH ARE COOKED IN ORANGE JUICE, WHICH GIVES THEM
A FRUITY FLAVOUR. THIS IS A PERFECT DISH FOR A VEGETARIAN.

SERVES	PREPARATION TIME	COOKING TIME	AUTO COOK
4	15 minutes	Cook on high 3 to 4 hours	4 to 6 hours

2 large or 4 small acorn squash

1 yellow pepper, deseeded and
   finely chopped

3 shallots, peeled and finely chopped

410-g/14½-oz can hearts of palm,
   drained, rinsed and chopped

3 medium tomatoes, deseeded and
   chopped

200 g/7 oz canned chick peas, drained
   and rinsed

1 red apple, cored and chopped

1 tbsp maple syrup or clear honey

Salt and freshly ground black pepper

250 ml/8 fl oz orange juice

2 tbsp cashew nuts, chopped

2 tbsp finely shredded fresh mint

1 Preheat the cooker on high while preparing ingredients. Cut the
squash in half and scoop out and discard the seeds. Mix all the
remaining ingredients together except for the orange juice, the
cashew nuts and 1 tablespoon of the shredded mint.

2 Spoon into the acorn halves and place in the cooking pot. Pour
around the orange juice. Cover and cook on high for 3 to 4 hours.
Serve sprinkled with the cashew nuts and the remaining mint.

MUSHROOM MEDLEY

IF YOU PREFER A THICKER SAUCE, AT THE END OF THE COOKING TIME, POUR THE LIQUOR INTO A SMALL PAN, BLEND 1 TABLESPOON OF CORNFLOUR WITH 2 TABLESPOONS OF WATER, STIR INTO THE COOKING LIQUOR AND BRING TO THE BOIL. COOK, STIRRING UNTIL THICKENED.

SERVES	PREPARATION TIME	COOKING TIME	AUTO COOK
4	15 minutes plus 20 minutes soaking	Cook on high 3 to 4 hours	4 to 6 hours

15 g/½ oz dried mushrooms

1 tbsp olive oil

4 shallots, peeled and cut into wedges

2–3 garlic cloves, peeled and crushed

1–2 red jalapeño chillies, deseeded and chopped

300 g/10 oz baby potatoes, scrubbed and diced

450 g/1 lb assorted mushrooms, including chanterelle, oyster, field, chestnut and button, wiped and sliced if large

4 plum tomatoes, peeled, deseeded and chopped

150 ml/¼ pt white wine

1 tbsp balsamic vinegar

1–2 tbsp chopped fresh basil, to garnish

Freshly shaved Parmesan cheese and warm crusty bread, to serve

1 Rinse the dried mushrooms in cold water, place in a small bowl and cover with almost boiling water and leave for 20 minutes. Drain, strain the soaking liquor and reserve. Slice any of the soaked mushrooms if large.

2 Preheat the cooker on high. Heat the oil in a frying pan and sauté the shallots, garlic and chillies for 3 minutes. Add the potatoes and sauté for 2 more minutes, then place in the cooking pot with all the mushrooms and the tomatoes. Heat the soaking liquor and white wine until almost boiling, then add the vinegar and pour over the mushrooms. Cover and cook on high for 3 to 4 hours. Sprinkle over the chopped basil and shaved Parmesan cheese and serve with the warm crusty bread. (This dish is delicious served cold as well.)

WINTER VEGETABLE CASSEROLE

THE BEAUTY OF PUY LENTILS, UNLIKE OTHER LENTILS, IS THAT THEY KEEP THEIR SHAPE THROUGHOUT THE COOKING PROCESS. MANY PEOPLE REGARD THEM AS THE BEST FLAVOURED, TOO.

SERVES	PREPARATION TIME	COOKING TIME	AUTO COOK
4 to 6	10 minutes	Cook on high 3 to 4 hours	4 to 7 hours

1 tbsp sunflower oil

1 onion, peeled and cut into wedges

2–3 garlic cloves, peeled and chopped

1–2 red serrano chillies, deseeded and chopped

1 tsp fennel seeds

$\frac{1}{2}$ tsp caraway seeds

2 medium carrots, peeled and sliced

1 acorn squash, peeled, deseeded, and diced

175 g/6 oz puy lentils, rinsed

300 g/10 oz diced turnip

1 fennel bulb, trimmed and sliced

750 ml/1$\frac{1}{4}$ pt vegetable stock

1 tsp dried mixed herbs

Few dashes Tabasco or hot sauce, to taste

Salt and freshly ground black pepper

2 tbsp chopped fresh parsley, to garnish

Goat's cheese, crumbled, to serve

1 Preheat the cooker on high. Heat the oil in a frying pan and sauté the onion, garlic, chillies, and fennel and caraway seeds for 3 minutes. Place in the cooking pot and add the rest of the ingredients except for the chopped parsley and cheese. Mix well.

2 Cook on high for 3 to 4 hours. Serve sprinkled with the chopped parsley and crumbled goat's cheese.

SLOW COOKED RED CABBAGE

RED CABBAGE IS A WONDERFUL VEGETABLE, REQUIRING LONG, SLOW COOKING – IDEAL FOR THE SLOW COOKER. ONCE YOU'VE TRIED THIS RECIPE, YOU WILL NEVER COOK RED CABBAGE ANY OTHER WAY.

SERVES	PREPARATION TIME	COOKING TIME	AUTO COOK
4 to 6	10 minutes	Cook on high 3 to 4 hours or low 6 to 8 hours	8 to 10 hours

1 red cabbage, about 900 g/2 lb

2 tbsp dark Muscovado sugar

1 large cooking apple, peeled, cored and chopped

2 tbsp red wine vinegar

Salt and freshly ground black pepper

½–1 tsp caraway seeds

250 ml/8 fl oz water

Soured cream, to serve

Preheat the cooker on high while preparing the ingredients. Cut the cabbage into quarters and discard the tough outer leaves and the central core. Finely shred the cabbage, then wash thoroughly in plenty of cold water until the water runs clear. Place in the cooking pot. Add the remaining ingredients except the soured cream. Stir, then cover and cook on high for 3 to 4 hours or low for 6 to 8 hours. Stir again, then serve with the soured cream.

THREE BEAN LASAGNA

USE PRE-COOKED LASAGNA SHEETS, BREAKING THEM TO FIT THE COOKING POT. ALTHOUGH THIS RECIPE USES BEANS, YOU CAN USE YOUR FAVOURITE MEAT LASAGNA RECIPE IN EXACTLY THE SAME WAY.

SERVES	PREPARATION TIME	COOKING TIME	AUTO COOK
4 to 6	10 minutes	Cook on low 4 to 5 hours	5 to 7 hours

1 tsp butter

1 tbsp oil

1 onion, peeled and chopped

2 garlic cloves, peeled and crushed

410-g/14½-oz can borlotti beans, drained and rinsed

300 g/10 oz canned cannellini beans, drained and rinsed

225 g/8 oz broad beans, thawed if frozen

410-g/14½-oz can chopped tomatoes

1 tsp dried oregano

Salt and freshly ground black pepper

8–12 sheets pre-cooked lasagna

600 ml/1 pt prepared béchamel sauce

50 g/2 oz freshly grated Parmesan cheese

Warm Italian bread; tossed green salad; tomato, black olive and basil salad, to serve

1 Preheat the slow cooker on high. Lightly grease the inside of the cooking pot with the butter. Heat the oil in a frying pan, then sauté the onion and garlic for 3 minutes. Add all the drained beans, the chopped tomatoes, dried oregano and the seasoning and mix well.

2 Arrange a layer of the bean mixture in the base of the cooking pot and cover with 2–3 lasagna sheets, breaking them to fit. Spoon over sufficient béchamel sauce to cover and sprinkle with a little of the grated Parmesan.

3 Continue layering, ending with a layer of cheese. Cover with the lid, reduce the cooker temperature to low and cook for 4 to 5 hours. Serve with plenty of warm Italian style bread, tossed green salad and a tomato and black olive with basil salad.

TUSCAN BEAN STEW

WHEN USING DRIED BEANS IT IS IMPORTANT THAT THEY ARE SOAKED OVERNIGHT IN WATER. RED KIDNEY BEANS SHOULD BE BOILED VIGOROUSLY FOR 10 MINUTES, DRAINED, RINSED AND USED AS DIRECTED.

SERVES	PREPARATION TIME	COOKING TIME	AUTO COOK
4 to 6	10 minutes plus overnight soaking	Cook on low 8 to 10 hours	12 to 14 hours

175 g/6 oz dried red kidney beans

175 g/6 oz dried borlotti beans

1 tbsp olive oil

1 red onion, peeled and cut into wedges

2–4 garlic cloves, peeled and chopped

1 small red jalapeño chilli, deseeded and chopped

1 fennel bulb, trimmed and cut into wedges

1 yellow pepper, deseeded and chopped

450 g/1 lb chopped plum tomatoes

2 tbsp tomato purée

Salt and freshly ground black pepper

1 tsp dried oregano

300 ml/½ pt vegetable stock

1 large courgette

2 tbsp chopped fresh parsley, to garnish

Warm crusty bread, soured cream and salad, to serve

1 Cover the dried beans with cold water and leave to soak overnight. Next day, drain the beans, rinse them if liked, place in a pan and cover with water. Bring to the boil and boil for 10 minutes, drain and reserve. Alternatively, simply drain, rinse and reserve.

2 Preheat the slow cooker on high while preparing ingredients. Heat the oil in a frying pan and sauté the onion, garlic and chilli for 3 minutes. Place in the cooking pot of the slow cooker, add the beans and all the remaining ingredients except for the courgette and stir well. Cover, reduce the heat and cook for 7½ hours.

3 Meanwhile, trim the courgette and peel if preferred and dice small. Cover with boiling water, then drain and add to the cooking pot 30 minutes before the end of the cooking time. Stir well, then continue to cook for another 30 minutes to 2 hours. Sprinkle with the parsley and serve with crusty bread, soured cream and salad.

6

DESSERTS

PEACH AND ALMOND CRUMBLE

CRUMBLES ARE ALWAYS A FAMILY FAVOURITE, AND ONE OF THE BEST WAYS OF
EATING THEM IS WITH PLENTY OF CREAM AND VANILLA ICE CREAM – HOW NAUGHTY
IS THAT? BUT HOW DELICIOUS! TRY IT WHEN YOU ARE FEELING REALLY DECADENT.

SERVES	PREPARATION TIME	COOKING TIME	AUTO COOK
4 to 6	10 minutes	Cook on low 4 to 5 hours	5 to 7 hours

1 tsp unsalted butter

6 ripe fresh peaches, skinned, stoned
   and sliced, or use canned sliced
   peaches

5 tbsp peach or orange juice, optional

1 tbsp honey, optional

½ tsp almond essence

100 g/4 oz wholemeal flour

50 g/2 oz porridge oats

25 g/1 oz ground blanched almonds

50 g/2 oz demerara sugar

1 tsp ground cinnamon

8 tbsp peanut butter

2 tbsp toasted flaked almonds

1 tsp caster sugar

Mint sprigs, to garnish

Cream, ice cream or frozen yoghurt,
   to serve

1 Preheat the cooker on high. Lightly grease a 1.5-litre/2½-pint heatproof dish with the butter, then either arrange the sliced fresh peaches in the base or drain the canned peaches, reserving 4 tablespoons of their juice, and place the canned peaches in the base.

2 If using fresh peaches, pour over the peach or orange juice and honey. If using canned fruit, use the canned juice. Sprinkle the fresh or canned peaches with the almond essence.

3 Place the flour, oats, almonds, sugar and cinnamon into a bowl, add the peanut butter and blend in. Sprinkle over the peaches and pat down lightly. Cover with the lid, then reduce the temperature to low and cook for 4 to 5 hours. Remove from the cooker, sprinkle with the flaked almonds and caster sugar, garnish with mint sprigs and serve with cream, ice cream or frozen yoghurt.

WASSAIL CUP

ALTHOUGH THIS CUP DOES NOT CONTAIN ANY ALCOHOL, IT CERTAINLY FEELS AS
THOUGH IT DOES. IT IS IDEAL TO SERVE TO THOSE WHO DO NOT DRINK ALCOHOL.

SERVES	PREPARATION TIME	COOKING TIME
6 to 8	5 minutes	Cook on low 2 to 3 hours

600 ml/1 pt clear apple juice

300 ml/½ pt apple cider

300 ml/½ pt black tea

2–4 tbsp demerara sugar, or to taste

1 sliced lemon

5 whole cloves

1 small piece root ginger, peeled
   and chopped

4 star anise

1 cinnamon stick, bruised

Apple slices and mint sprigs, to
   decorate

Preheat the cooker on high. Place all the ingredients into the cooking pot and cover with the lid. Cook on low for 2 to 3 hours, then serve in heatproof glasses, decorated with apple slices and mint sprigs.

CHOCOLATE BRIOCHE PUDDING

THIS DESSERT IS REAL COMFORT FOOD – THE BIGGEST PROBLEM IS THAT IT IS SO DELICIOUS YOU HAVE TO KEEP GOING BACK FOR MORE.

SERVES	PREPARATION TIME	COOKING TIME
4 to 6	15 minutes	Cook on high 3 to 4 hours

2 tbsp butter
3 individual brioches or ½ large brioche
100 g/4 oz chopped stoned dates
2 tbsp light soft brown sugar, or to taste
100 g/4 oz plain dark chocolate, melted
3 medium eggs
300 ml/½ pt skimmed milk
1–2 tsp icing sugar, sifted
Cream, to serve

1 Preheat the slow cooker on high for 20 minutes. Lightly smear the inside of a 1.2-litre/2-pint heatproof dish with a little of the butter. Slice the brioches and spread with the softened butter. Arrange in the buttered dish, scatter over the dates and sugar to taste. Stir the chocolate until smooth, then pour over the brioche and dates.

2 Beat the eggs with the milk, then pour over the brioche mixture. Place the dish in the cooker and pour hot water around it so that the water level comes halfway up the dish. Cover with the lid and cook on high for 3 to 4 hours or until a skewer inserted into the centre comes out clean. Sprinkle with the icing sugar and serve with cream.

PEARS IN RUM AND MAPLE SYRUP

SELECT EVENLY SHAPED PEARS, ONES THAT WILL STAND UPRIGHT, FOR THIS DISH. CONFERENCE PEARS ARE AN IDEAL CHOICE.

SERVES	PREPARATION TIME	COOKING TIME
4	10 minutes	Cook on high 3 to 5 hours

4 firm pears
4 tbsp maple syrup
4 tbsp rum
300 ml/½ pt water
2 strips pared orange rind
1 cinnamon stick, bruised
Cream and sweet biscuits, to serve
Extra orange rind and cinnamon stick, to decorate

1 Preheat the slow cooker on high. Peel the pears, keeping them whole and, if possible, keeping the stalk intact. Place in the cooking pot. Heat the maple syrup, rum and water and bring to the boil.

2 Pour over the pears and add the orange rind and cinnamon stick. Cover and cook on high for 3 to 5 hours, turning the pears occasionally so they are coated in the syrup. Remove from the cooking pot and place in a serving dish. Pour the syrup into a pan, discarding the orange rind and cinnamon stick, and bring to the boil. Boil vigorously for 8 to 10 minutes until reduced slightly. Pour over the pears and serve with cream and sweet biscuits and decorated with extra orange rind and cinnamon sticks.

SUNSET APPLES

IT IS IMPORTANT TO USE FIRM APPLES. YOU NEED A VARIETY THAT DO NOT BREAK
DOWN AND BECOME FLUFFY DURING COOKING; OTHERWISE, YOU WILL FIND THAT
THE APPLES WILL COLLAPSE DURING THE LONG COOKING.

SERVES	PREPARATION TIME	COOKING TIME
4	10 minutes	Cook on low 2 to 3 hours

1 to 2 tbsp butter

4 large evenly shaped cooking apples

25 g/1 oz dried cranberries

25 g/1 oz hazelnuts, chopped

3 tbsp light soft brown sugar

3 tbsp redcurrant jelly or seedless
   raspberry jam

4 fresh bay leaves, to garnish

Cream, to serve

1 Preheat the cooker on high. Lightly smear the cooking pot with a little
of the butter. Core the apples and rinse. Mix together the cranberries,
hazelnuts and sugar and use this mixture to fill the centre of each
apple. Place in the cooking pot and dot with the remaining butter.

2 Heat the jelly or jam with 3 tablespoons of water, stir until smooth,
then pour over the apples. Cover and cook on low for 2 to 4 hours.
Serve garnished with the bay leaves and with cream.

MAPLE SYRUP PUDDING

WHEN COOKING A SPONGE-STYLE PUDDING IN THE SLOW COOKER, IT IS
IMPORTANT THAT THE COOKER IS PREHEATED ON HIGH FOR 20 MINUTES
AND THE PUDDING IS COOKED FOR THE RECOMMENDED TIME.

SERVES	PREPARATION TIME	COOKING TIME
6	10 minutes	Cook on high 5 to 7 hours

1 tsp butter

6 tbsp maple syrup

100 g/4 oz softened butter
   or margarine

100 g/4 oz caster sugar

2 medium eggs

½ tsp vanilla essence

100 g/4 oz self-raising flour*

25 g/1 oz ground blanched almonds

Cream or custard, to serve

1 Preheat the slow cooker on high for 20 minutes. Lightly grease a
900-ml/1½-pint pudding basin with the butter and line the base with
a small circle of greaseproof paper. Pour 4 tablespoons of the syrup in
the base of the basin and reserve.

2 Place all the ingredients except the remaining syrup into a mixing bowl
and beat until combined, then spoon into the basin and level the top.
Cover loosely with a double sheet of tinfoil. Place in the cooking pot of
the slow cooker and pour around sufficient water to come halfway up
the side of the basin. Cover with the lid and cook on high for 5 to 7
hours. Turn out onto a serving plate and discard the greaseproof
paper circle. Heat the remaining syrup and pour over the pudding,
then serve with the cream or custard.

*If using plain flour, add 1¼ tsp baking powder and ¼ tsp salt.

CHOCOLATE AND ORANGE PUDDING

YOU CAN VARY THE FLAVOURS IN THIS WICKED PUDDING – TRY ADDING SOME GROUND CINNAMON OR CRUSHED CARDAMOM PODS – THEN YOU COULD ALSO ADD SOME CHOCOLATE CHIPS, DRIED CHERRIES OR EVEN SOME RAISINS.

SERVES	PREPARATION TIME	COOKING TIME
6	15 minutes	Cook on high 5 to 7 hours

100 g/4 oz plain dark chocolate

100 g/4 oz margarine or butter, softened

100 g/4 oz light soft brown sugar

2 tbsp grated orange rind

2 medium eggs, beaten

100 g/4 oz self-raising flour*

25 g/1 oz ground blanched almonds

2 tbsp cocoa powder, sifted

1–2 tbsp orange juice

2 tsp icing sugar

Chocolate or orange sauce, or cream and fresh redcurrants or orange segments, to serve

1 Preheat the slow cooker on high for 20 minutes. Take a 900-ml/ 1½-pint heatproof pudding basin, lightly butter and line the base with a circle of greaseproof paper. Break the chocolate into small pieces and place over a pan of gently simmering water and heat, stirring occasionally until the chocolate has melted. Stir until smooth, reserve.

2 Cream the margarine or butter with the sugar and orange rind until light and fluffy, then gradually beat in the eggs, adding a little flour after each addition. When all the eggs have been added, stir in the melted chocolate followed by the remaining flour, ground almonds and cocoa powder. Mix with the orange juice to give a smooth dropping consistency. Spoon into the prepared basin and level the top. Cover loosely with a double sheet of tinfoil.

3 Place in the cooking pot of the slow cooker and pour around sufficient water to come halfway up the side of the basin. Cover with the lid and cook on high for 5 to 7 hours. Turn out, discard the greaseproof circle and serve dusted with icing sugar, along with chocolate or orange sauce, or with cream and fresh redcurrants or orange segments.

*If using plain flour, add 1¼ tsp baking powder and ¼ tsp salt.

CREAMY RICE PUDDING

REMEMBER TO RINSE THE RICE THOROUGHLY BEFORE USING, ESPECIALLY IF USING PUDDING RICE; OTHERWISE, THE PUDDING WILL BE A LITTLE STARCHY.

SERVES	PREPARATION TIME	COOKING TIME	AUTO COOK
4	5 minutes	Cook on high 3 to 4 hours or low 4 to 6 hours	4 to 7 hours

1 tsp butter

50 g/2 oz pudding rice or easy-cook long-grain rice

2 tbsp caster sugar

150 ml/¼ pt evaporated milk

900 ml/1½ pt semi-skimmed milk

2 tsp grated orange rind

A little freshly grated nutmeg

Jam or marmalade sauce, to serve

Preheat the slow cooker on high; grease the cooking pot with the butter. Rinse the rice and place in the cooking pot. Add all the remaining ingredients (except the accompaniments) and stir well. Cover and cook on high for 3 to 4 hours. Stir, then serve with either jam or marmalade sauce.

LEMON AND ORANGE CHEESE

BECAUSE OF THE LONG SLOW COOKING, THERE IS NO DANGER OF THE CHEESE CURDLING, HOWEVER DO NOT BE TEMPTED TO SHORTCUT AND NOT USE A BASIN.

MAKES	PREPARATION TIME	COOKING TIME
450 g/1 lb	10 minutes	Cook on low 3 to 4 hours

1 lemon, preferably unwaxed or organic

1 orange, preferably unwaxed or organic

100 g/4 oz unsalted butter

450 g/1 lb caster sugar

4 medium eggs

1 Preheat the cooker on high. Finely grate the rind from the lemon and orange and squeeze out the juice. Place in a non-reactive pan, add the butter, then stir in the sugar. Heat gently until the butter has melted and the sugar dissolved, then allow to cool.

2 When cool, beat the eggs into the sweetened juice, then pour into a 1.2-litre/2-pint pudding basin and cover with tinfoil. Place in the slow cooker and pour in sufficient water to come halfway up the sides of the basin. Reduce the temperature and cook on low for 3 to 4 hours or until thickened. (If possible, stir occasionally during cooking.) Stir well, then pot in sterilized warm, small, glass jars and cover with a wax disc. When cold, cover with cellophane lids. Store in the refrigerator and use within 1 month.

BLUEBERRY MUFFIN BAKE

AS WITH CONVENTIONAL STYLE MUFFINS IT IS IMPORTANT THAT YOU DO NOT OVERMIX THE INGREDIENTS, OTHERWISE THE FINISHED BAKE WILL NOT BE AS LIGHT AS IT SHOULD BE.

SERVES	PREPARATION TIME	COOKING TIME
6	10 minutes	Cook on high 3 to 4 hours

75 g/3 oz unsalted butter

75 g/3 oz light Muscovado sugar

100 g/4 oz wholemeal self-raising flour*

100 g/4 oz white self-raising flour*

1 tsp ground cinnamon

175 g/6 oz fresh blueberries

50 g/2 oz pecans, chopped

2 medium eggs, beaten

6–8 tbsp buttermilk

1–2 tsp demerara sugar

Cream or mascarpone cheese, to serve

1 Preheat the cooker on high. Lightly butter a 1.5-litre/2½-pint heatproof dish that will sit in the cooking pot, then place the remaining butter in a pan with the sugar and heat until melted. Sift the flours and ground cinnamon into a mixing bowl, then stir in the bran left in the sieve from the wholemeal flour. Add the melted butter mixture and stir until blended. Add the blueberries and pecans, stir, then beat in the egg and sufficient buttermilk to give a soft dropping consistency. Take care not to overmix.

2 Spoon into the buttered dish, sprinkle the top with the demerara sugar and place in the cooking pot. Pour around sufficient water to come halfway up the sides of the dish. Cover and cook on high for 3 to 4 hours. Serve with cream or mascarpone cheese.

* If using plain flour add 3 tsp baking powder and ½ tsp salt.

AUTUMN RELISH

UNLIKE OTHER RELISHES, THIS ONE DOES NOT NEED TO MATURE BUT CAN BE
USED IMMEDIATELY. THIS IS BECAUSE OF THE LONG SLOW COOKING.

MAKES	PREPARATION TIME	COOKING TIME
1.25 kg/2½ lb	15 minutes	Cook on high 6 to 8 hours

675 g/1½ lb cooking apples, peeled,
  cored and chopped

2 large onions, peeled and chopped

1–2 red serrano chillies, deseeded
  and chopped

225 g/8 oz firm but ripe pears, peeled,
  cored and chopped

1 red pepper, deseeded and chopped

2–4 garlic cloves, peeled and crushed

450 g/1 lb light soft brown sugar

225 g/8 oz dried apricots, chopped

1 tsp ground ginger

1 tsp ground allspice

150 ml/¼ pt white wine vinegar

Fresh herb sprigs, to garnish, optional

Preheat the cooker on high. Place all the ingredients in the cooking pot or large pan and heat, stirring, until the sugar has dissolved. (If using a pan, transfer to the cooking pot.) Cover and cook for 6 to 8 hours, stirring occasionally. (Do ensure that you replace the lid firmly so that the liquid does not evaporate.) Stir well, then spoon into sterilized warm, glass jars and cover with a waxed disc. Once cold, cover with cellophane or plastic screw-top lids. Use within 3 months. Garnish with fresh herb sprigs if liked.

STICKY DATE AND TOFFEE PUDDING

THIS PUDDING IS FOR THOSE WITH A SERIOUS SWEET TOOTH. IT IS ABSOLUTELY
DELICIOUS, WITH A REALLY RICH, STICKY BASE UNDER THE LIGHT FLUFFY SPONGE.

SERVES	PREPARATION TIME	COOKING TIME
6	15 minutes	Cook on high 5 to 7 hours

175 g/6 oz unsalted butter, softened

175 g/6 oz light Muscovado sugar

2 medium eggs, beaten

100 g/4 oz self-raising flour*

75 g/3 oz chopped stoned dates

25 g/1 oz plain dark chocolate, melted

2 tsp icing sugar, sifted

Cream or vanilla ice cream, to serve

1 Preheat the cooker on high. Lightly butter a 1.2-litre/2-pint heatproof dish that will fit in the cooking pot. Beat together the butter and sugar until light and creamy, then place 3 tablespoons of the mixture in the dish and spread over the whole base. Beat the eggs gradually into the remaining butter and sugar mixture, adding a little flour after each addition. When all the eggs have been added, add the remaining flour, then stir in the dates and melted chocolate. Spoon into the dish and cover with a sheet of tinfoil.

2 Place in the cooker and pour sufficient hot water around to come halfway up the sides of the dish. Cover and cook on high for 5 hours. Serve the bake sprinkled with the icing sugar and with either cream or ice cream.

* If using plain flour, add 1 ¼ tsp baking power and ¼ tsp salt.

◄ Autumn Relish

CHRISTMAS GROG

WHEN IT IS COLD AND BLUSTERY, WHAT COULD BE BETTER THAN A GLASS OF WARM SPICY WINE? IT WILL WARM YOU RIGHT THROUGH TO YOUR TOES.

SERVES	PREPARATION TIME	COOKING TIME
8 to 10	5 minutes	Cook on low 8 to 9 hours

2 medium oranges

5 cloves

5 cardamom pods, lightly bruised

50-75 g/2–3 oz light soft brown sugar

2 cinnamon sticks, bruised

1 bottle Claret wine

150 ml/¼ pt brandy

Preheat the cooker on high. Rinse or scrub the oranges and stud 1 with the whole cloves. Place the studded orange in the cooking pot and cook on high for 1 hour. Add the remaining ingredients except for the other orange. Cover and reduce the temperature to low and cook for 7 hours. Slice the remaining orange and float on top of the wine. Remove the whole orange and cinnamon sticks, then serve in heatproof glasses with the orange slices floating on top.

PLUM PUDDING

SOME MIGHT WISH TO KEEP THIS VERY RICH PUDDING FOR SPECIAL OCCASIONS, SUCH AS CHRISTMAS OR THANKSGIVING, BUT THAT WOULD BE A PITY. IT IS SO GOOD, WHY NOT SERVE IT ON A REGULAR BASIS?

SERVES	PREPARATION TIME	COOKING TIME
8	15 minutes	Cook on high 8 to 12 hours

100 g/4 oz unsalted butter, softened

100 g/4 oz dark Muscovado sugar

1 tbsp grated orange rind

1 tbsp black treacle

2 large eggs, beaten

50 g/2 oz wholemeal self-raising flour*

175 g/6 oz raisins

175 g/6 oz golden sultanas

50 g/2 oz dried cranberries or ready-to-eat apricots, chopped

75 g/3 oz glacé cherries, chopped

1 tsp ground mixed spice

½ tsp ground ginger

100 g/4 oz fresh wholemeal breadcrumbs

2-3 tbsp brandy, sherry, or orange juice

Brandy butter or cream, to serve

1 Lightly oil and line the base of a 1.2-litre/2-pint pudding basin with a small circle of greaseproof paper and set aside. Beat together the butter, sugar and orange rind until light and fluffy, then stir in the black treacle. Gradually add the eggs, a little at a time, beating well and adding a spoonful of flour after each addition.

2 When all the eggs have been added, stir in any remaining flour and the rest of the ingredients except for the brandy, sherry or fruit juice. Mix well, then add sufficient brandy, sherry or juice to give a soft dropping consistency. Spoon into the prepared basin and cover with a sheet of greaseproof paper and double sheet of tinfoil folded with a pleat in the centre to allow for expansion. Place on a sling of foil for ease of lifting.

3 Place in the cooking pot of the cooker and pour around sufficient hot water to come three-quarters of the way up the basin. Cover with the lid and cook on high for 8 to 12 hours, topping up the water as necessary. Remove and either serve immediately with brandy butter or cream or recover and store in a cool dry place until required. (Reheat in the cooker with water poured around as before for at least 4 hours.)

* If using plain flour add ¾ tsp baking powder and pinch of salt.

CANDIED CHERRY AND GINGER BREAD AND BUTTER PUDDING

YOU CAN USE FRUITED BREAD, OR ORDINARY WHITE OR BROWN BREAD FOR THIS RECIPE. TRY IT WITH SLICED BRIOCHE, OR EVEN A SEEDED LOAF. WHICHEVER YOU USE, YOU WILL BE DELIGHTED WITH THE FINISHED DISH.

SERVES	PREPARATION TIME	COOKING TIME
4	15 minutes	Cook on high 3 to 5 hours

2 tbsp butter, softened

6–8 slices fruit loaf

50 g/2 oz glacé cherries, chopped

50 g/2 oz stem or crystallized ginger, chopped

50 g/2 oz dried blueberries or cranberries

1 tbsp grated orange rind

1 tsp ground ginger

2 tbsp maple syrup

2 large eggs

250 ml/8 fl oz single cream

Caster sugar, for sprinkling

Cream or custard, to serve

1 Preheat the cooker on high. Lightly butter a 1.2-litre/2-pint ovenproof dish that will sit in your cooking pot and set aside. Spread the bread with the remaining butter and cut into small triangles. Arrange half of the bread in the base of the dish and sprinkle with the cherries, ginger, blueberries or cranberries and finally the grated orange rind. Top with the remaining buttered bread.

2 Blend the ginger and maple syrup together, then beat in the eggs followed by the cream. Pour over the bread and let stand for 30 minutes. Place in the cooking pot, using a tinfoil sling for ease of lifting. Pour sufficient hot water to come halfway up the sides of the dish. Cover and cook on high for 3 to 5 hours or until the custard has set. Sprinkle with sugar and serve with cream or custard.

SPICY WINTER COMPOTE

FRUIT, WHETHER FRESH OR DRIED, COOKED IN THE SLOW COOKER RETAINS ALL ITS NATURAL FLAVOURS; THE SPICES, WINE OR JUICES USED IN THE COOKING SLOWLY BLEND INTO THE FRUIT.

SERVES	PREPARATION TIME	COOKING TIME
6 to 8	5 minutes	Cook on low 7 to 8 hours

450 g/1 lb mixed dried fruit

100 g/4 oz raisins

2–4 tbsp light soft brown sugar

4 whole cloves

½ tsp ground allspice

¼ tsp freshly grated nutmeg

1 cinnamon stick, bruised

2 strips thinly pared lemon rind

250 ml/8 fl oz white wine

300 ml/½ pt orange juice

Mascarpone cheese or plain yoghurt, to serve

Preheat the slow cooker on high. Rinse the mixed dried fruit and place in the cooking pot with the raisins; sprinkle in the sugar, the spices and the lemon rind. If you have a sweet tooth, increase the sugar up to 4 tablespoons. Pour over the white wine and orange juice, then cover and cook on low for 7 to 8 hours before serving with either mascarpone cheese or yoghurt.

CRÈME BRÛLÉE

IF DESIRED, YOU CAN PUT SOME FRESH FRUITS IN THE BASE OF THE DISH BEFORE POURING IN THE CUSTARD. USE FRUITS THAT ARE FAIRLY FIRM IN TEXTURE; OTHERWISE, THEY MAY COLLAPSE TOO MUCH DURING THE LONG COOKING.

SERVES	PREPARATION TIME	COOKING TIME
4	15 minutes	Cook on low 3 to 6 hours

3 medium eggs
175 g/6 oz caster sugar
1 tsp vanilla essence
250 ml/8 fl oz single cream
120 ml/4 fl oz double cream
120 ml/4 fl oz milk

1 Preheat the cooker on high. Beat the eggs with 3 tablespoons of the sugar and the vanilla essence until thoroughly blended. Slightly warm the cream and milk, then beat into the egg mixture. Strain into 4 to 6 individual ramekin dishes, ensuring that they fit inside the cooking pot, then place in the pot.

2 Pour around sufficient hot water to come three-quarters of the way up the sides of the dishes. Cover and cook on low for 3 hours or until set. Remove and allow to cool.

3 Sprinkle the tops with the remaining caster sugar. Place under a preheated grill and cook until the sugar melts and caramelizes. You will need to turn the dishes to ensure that the sugar melts evenly. Remove from the grill, cool, then chill until required.

APPLE AND CRANBERRY PUDDING

ANY DRIED FRUIT, SUCH AS CHOPPED APRICOTS, PRUNES, MANGO, PAPAYA, CHERRIES, OR A MIXTURE OF FRUITS, CAN BE USED IN PLACE OF THE CRANBERRIES IN THIS PUDDING.

SERVES	PREPARATION TIME	COOKING TIME
6	15 minutes	Cook on high 4 to 6 hours

120 ml/4 fl oz sunflower oil
175 g/6 oz light soft brown sugar
2 medium eggs
1 tbsp grated orange rind
175 g/6 oz self-raising wholemeal flour*
1 tsp ground cinnamon
75 g/3 oz dried cranberries
1 cooking apple, peeled, cored and chopped
1–2 tbsp orange juice
Cream or custard, to serve

Preheat the slow cooker on high for 20 minutes. Lightly oil a 900-ml/1½-pint pudding basin and place a small round of greaseproof paper in the base. Beat the sugar, oil and eggs together; then add the orange rind, flour and cinnamon. Beat well, then stir in the cranberries and apple with sufficient orange juice to give a dropping consistency. Spoon into the prepared basin and cover with a double sheet of tinfoil. Place in the slow cooker cooking pot. Cook on high for 4 to 6 hours, then turn out and serve with cream or custard.

* If using plain flour, add 2 tsp baking powder and $\frac{1}{4}$ tsp salt.

▶ Crème Brûlée

CHOCOLATE FONDUE

THERE IS SOMETHING REALLY DECADENT ABOUT CHOCOLATE, SO WHEN YOU ARE IN NEED OF A CHOCOLATE FIX WHY NOT GO COMPLETELY OVERBOARD AND INDULGE IN THIS RICH AND LUSCIOUS CHOCOLATE FONDUE?

SERVES	PREPARATION TIME	COOKING TIME
6 to 8	5 minutes	Cook on low 1 to 3 hours

350 g/12 oz plain dark chocolate

250 ml/8 fl oz double cream

2 tbsp maple syrup, or to taste

3–4 tbsp brandy or Cointreau

Assorted fresh fruits and small sweet firm cakes, for dipping

Preheat the cooker on high. Break the chocolate into pieces and place in the cooking pot with the cream, maple syrup and brandy or Cointreau. Cover and cook for 1 hour or until the chocolate has melted. Stir until smooth, then either use immediately with the fruits and cakes for dipping or keep on low for up to 2 hours.

GINGERBREAD

ALTHOUGH THE TOP OF THIS GINGERBREAD IS NOT CRISP, THE FLAVOUR AND TEXTURE IS SUPERB – TRY IT FOR YOURSELF AND SEE.

MAKES	PREPARATION TIME	COOKING TIME
10 to 12	15 minutes	Cook on high 6 to 8 hours

175 g/6 oz light soft brown sugar

100 g/4 oz unsalted butter

75 g/3 oz golden syrup

75 g/3 oz black treacle

2–3 tsp ground ginger

100 g/4 oz plain flour

100 g/4 oz self-raising flour

1 ¼ tsp baking powder

Pinch salt

1 large egg

120 ml/4 fl oz milk

½ tsp bicarbonate of soda

1 Preheat cooker on high while preparing the ingredients. Lightly oil and base line a 18-cm/7-inch round cake tin or a 1.25-kg/2½-pint dish. Heat the sugar, butter, golden syrup and black treacle in a saucepan until melted, stirring until smooth. Sift the ground ginger with the flours, baking powder and salt into a mixing bowl, then beat in the melted sugar mixture. Cool slightly, then beat in the egg and stir well.

2 Warm the milk, stir in the bicarbonate of soda and stir into the mixture. Mix well, then pour into the prepared cake tin and place on top of an upturned ramekin or other small, heatproof dish.

3 Pour around sufficient hot water to come halfway up the sides of the cake tin.

4 Cover and cook on high for 6 to 8 hours. Remove from the tin, cool slightly, then invert onto a wire cooling rack. Cut into slices to serve. Store in an airtight container.

◄ Chocolate Fondue